Welcome to the Reading/Writing Workshop

Explore new ideas!

Become an expert writer!

Read and reread exciting literature and informational texts!

Use what you have learned to unlock the Wonders of reading!

Go Digital! www.connected.mcgraw-hill.com
Explore your Interactive Reading/Writing Workshop.

(t)Inaki Relanzon/naturepl.com; (rt) Andy Rouse/The Image Bank/Getty Images; (rb) Daniel Moreton; (b) Nathan Love

McGraw Hill Education

Bothell, WA • Chicago, IL • Columbus, OH • New York, NY

Cover and Title Pages: Nathan Love

www.mheonline.com/readingwonders C

The McGraw-Hill Companies

McGraw Hill Education

Send all inquiries to:
McGraw-Hill Education
Two Penn Plaza
New York, New York 10121

ISBN: 978-0-02-119585-5
MHID: 0-02-119585-4

Printed in the United States of America.

8 9 DOW 17 16 15 14

McGraw-Hill Reading Wonders

CCSS Reading/Language Arts Program

Program Authors

Diane August
Donald R. Bear
Janice A. Dole
Jana Echevarria
Douglas Fisher
David Francis
Vicki Gibson
Jan Hasbrouck
Margaret Kilgo
Jay McTighe
Scott G. Paris
Timothy Shanahan
Josefina V. Tinajero

McGraw Hill Education

Bothell, WA • Chicago, IL • Columbus, OH • New York, NY

Unit 4

Animals Everywhere

The Big Idea

Week 1 • Animal Features 12

Week 2 • Animals Together 32

Go Digital! www.mheonline.com/readingwonders

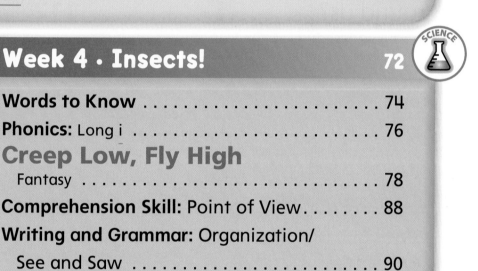

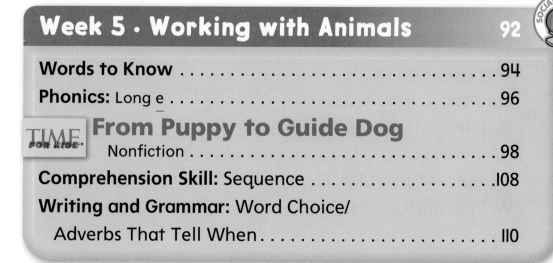

(t) Andy Rouse/The Image Bank/Getty Images; (b) Daniel Moreton

Unit 5 Figure It Out

The Big Idea

Go Digital! www.mheonline.com/readingwonders

Unit 6 Together We Can!

The Big Idea

(t) Gynux; (b) Masterfile

Week 3 · Weather Together 256

Week 4 · Sharing Traditions 276

Week 5 · Celebrate America! 296

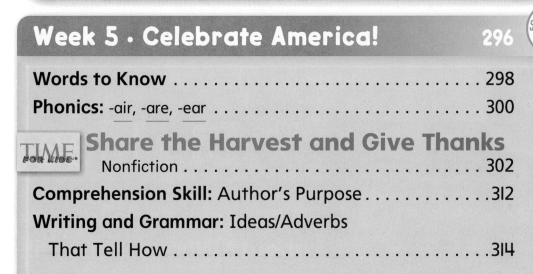

Unit 4

Animals Everywhere

MIYAKO/a.collectionRF/Getty Images

The Big Idea

What animals do you know about? What are they like?

Animals on the Go

Animals are on the go,
Some moving fast, some moving slow.

Crabs and spiders like to crawl,
A turtle hardly moves at all.

Elephants stomp when they pass,
But snakes just slither through the grass.

Kangaroos and rabbits hop,
BOING BOING BOUNCE—

Do they EVER stop?

—by Allegra Perrot

Weekly Concept Animal Features

Essential Question

How do animals' bodies help them?

Go Digital!

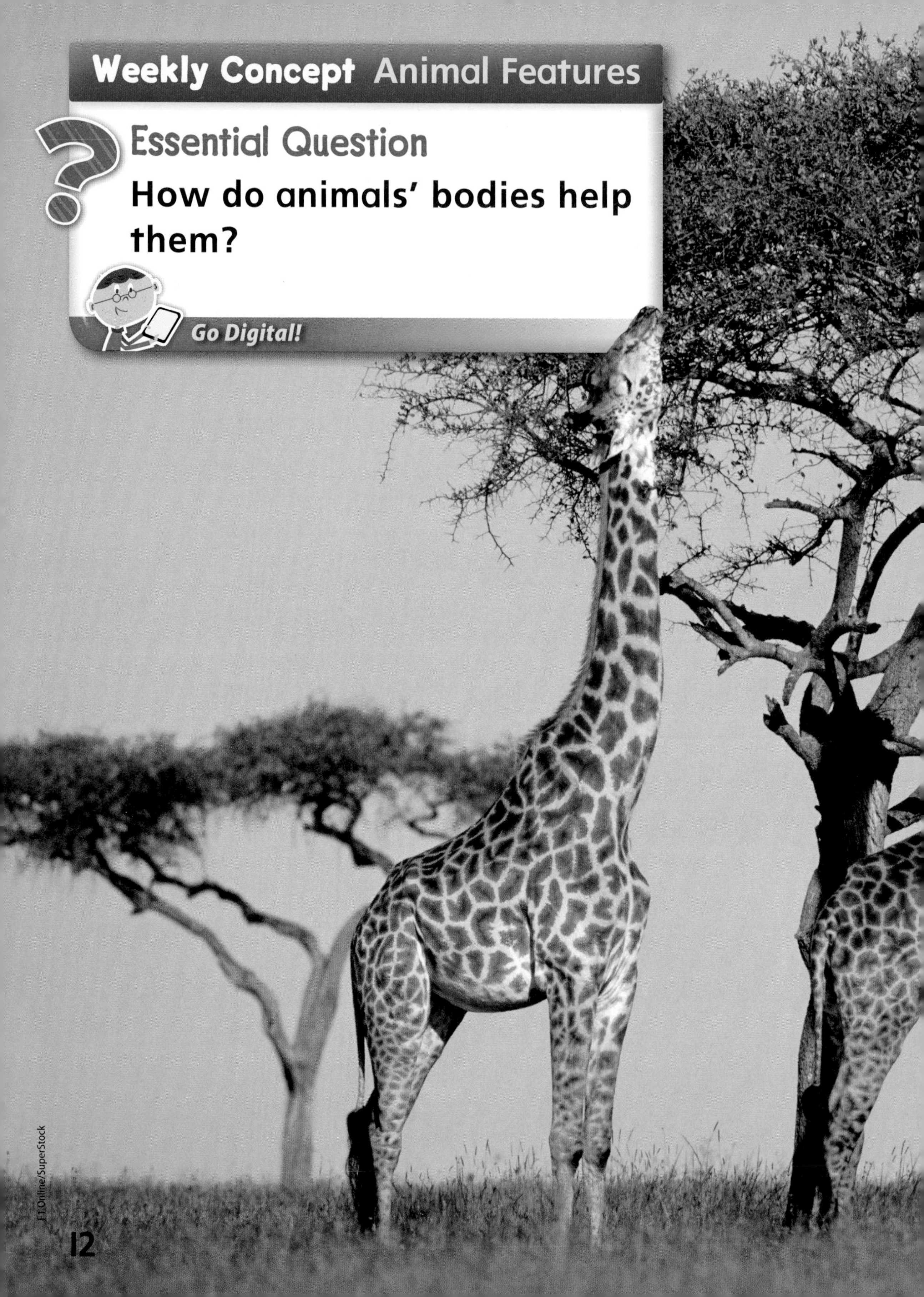

F1Online/SuperStock

Creature Features

COLLABORATE

Talk About It

What part of the body is helping these giraffes?

Words to Know

about

Did you see this book **about** bats?

animal

This **animal** has a trunk.

carry

It's easy to **carry** a little pet.

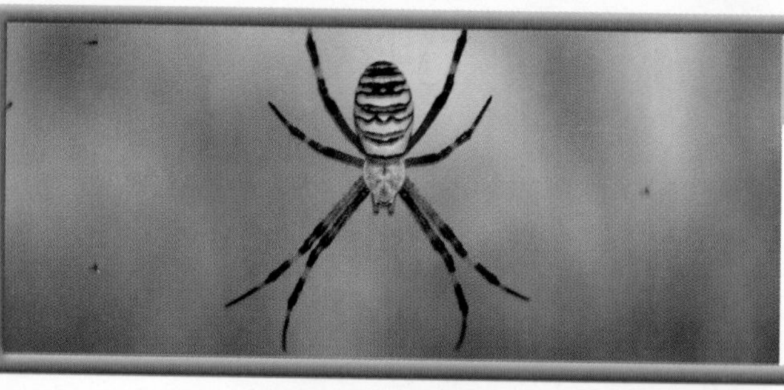

eight

A spider has **eight** legs.

give

I **give** my dog some water.

our

Our parrots like to talk.

special

Penguins move in a **special** way.

splendid

A peacock has a **splendid** tail.

Your Turn

Read the sentence for each word. Then make up another sentence.

Go Digital! Use the online visual glossary

(t to b, l to r) SVGiles/Flickr Open/Getty Images; Jack Weinberg/Image Source/PunchStock; Image Source/PunchStock; imagebroker.net/SuperStock; Juniors Bildarchiv/age fotostock; IT Stock/PunchStock/Getty Images; Digital Vision/Getty Images; Corbis/SuperStock

Long a

The letters a, ai, and ay make the long a sound in **apron**, **paint**, and **gray**.

may	**play**	**days**
paid	**stained**	**trains**
clay	**mail**	**staying**
April	**agent**	**basic**

Read Together

Will David stay inside if it rains?

David and Ray may play with trains.

Your Turn

Look for these words with long a in "A Tale of a Tail."

tail	**Ray**	**day**
April	**swayed**	**way**
wailed	**explained**	

CCSS **Genre** Folktale

Essential Question

How do animals' bodies help them?

Read about how a beaver's tail helps him.

Go Digital!

Valeria Cis

A Tale of a Tail

Long ago, there lived a beaver named Ray.

Ray was quite proud of his nice thick tail. He spent a lot of time brushing and fluffing it.

Valeria Cis

"I have a **splendid** tail," Ray bragged. "It is the best tail that an **animal** can have!"

One fine day in April, Ray went out.

"It is a nice day to chop wood," he said. So Ray got his ax. He chop, chop, chopped a big tree **eight** times.

Valeria Cis

The big tree swayed this way and that. Then it fell—on top of Ray's tail! Ray tugged and tugged at his tail. He gasped when he pulled it out.

"My tail is flat!" Ray wailed.

The sun looked down at him. She could tell that Ray felt bad **about** his tail.

Valeria Cis

"A flat tail will help you swim fast," the sun explained. "A flat tail can send a signal, too. Just slap it on the water."

That made Ray happy.

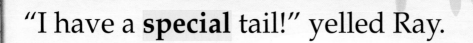

"I have a **special** tail!" yelled Ray.

Then Ray slapped his tail on the water. SLAP, SLAP, SLAP!

His pals came running. "Do you want **our** help?" they asked.

Valeria Cis

“I want to **give** you a ride,”
said Ray. “Hop on my tail.
I will **carry** you across the lake.”

And happy Ray swam off as fast
as a fish!

Make Connections

How did Ray’s new tail help him?

Sequence

The **sequence** is the order of events in a story. Think about what happens first, next, then, and last in the folktale.

Find Text Evidence

Find out what happens first in the story.

page 20

Long ago, there lived a beaver named Ray.

Ray was quite proud of his nice thick tail. He spent a lot of time brushing and fluffing it.

Valeria Cis

First

Ray likes his thick, bushy tail a lot.

Next

A tree falls and makes Ray's tail flat. He is sad.

Then

The sun explains how a flat tail will help Ray.

Last

Ray's flat tail helps him send a signal, swim fast, and give his pals a ride.

COLLABORATE

Your Turn

Talk about the sequence of events in "A Tale of a Tail."

Go Digital! *Use the interactive graphic organizer*

Readers to...

Word Choice Craig used words to tell what sounds the animals made.

Craig's Folktale

Bees were in their hive. Buzz!
Bear was hungry. Yum, yum!
"I'll get some honey," he said.
Buzz, buzz! "My paw was
stung!" Bear yelled.

Your Turn

COLLABORATE

Tell what sound words Craig chose.

Read Together

Writers

Was and Were Use **was** to tell about one person, animal, or thing in the past. Use **were** to tell about more than one person, animal, or thing in the past.

Bees **were** in their hive.

Bear **was** hungry.

Your Turn

- Find another sentence with **was** in Craig's folktale.
- Write new sentences with **was** and **were**.

Valeria Cis

Weekly Concept Animals Together

Essential Question

How do animals help each other?

Go Digital!

NHPA/Photoshot

Team Up!

Talk About It

How do the bird and the hippo help each other?

Words to Know

because

This team will win **because** it is fast.

blue

The geese fly in the **blue** sky.

into

They go **into** the water together.

or

Do you think the deer will stay **or** run?

other

One animal cleans the **other**.

Read Together

small

Small ants can carry very big bits.

danger

Mom keeps her cub out of **danger**.

partner

A **partner** is a big help.

COLLABORATE

Your Turn

Read the sentence for each word. Then make up another sentence.

Go Digital! *Use the online visual glossary*

(t to b, l to r) imagebroker.net/SuperStock; age fotostock/SuperStock; Minden Pictures/SuperStock; Image Source/Getty Images; Westend61/SuperStock; Gail Shumway/Photographer's Choice/Getty Images; Eric Baccega/age fotostock/SuperStock; Somos/SuperStock

Long e

The letters e, ee, ea, and ie make the long e sound in **he**, **bees**, **eat**, and **chief**.

me	**see**	**each**
she	**leaf**	**peek**
brief	**treated**	**thief**
meeting	**green**	**beast**

We peeked at Jean's hives in the field.

She told us, "Each bee works hard."

Your Turn

Look for these words with long e in "A Team of Fish."

team	**creeks**	**deep**	**seas**
the	**each**	**eat**	**be**
chief	**reason**	**neat**	**keep**

CCSS **Genre** Nonfiction

Essential Question

How do animals help each other?

Read about how some fish help each other.

Go Digital!

Martin Strmiska/Alamy

A Team of Fish

Fish swim in lakes and creeks. Fish swim in deep **blue** seas **or** oceans.

Let's dive **into** the water. Let's look at fish!

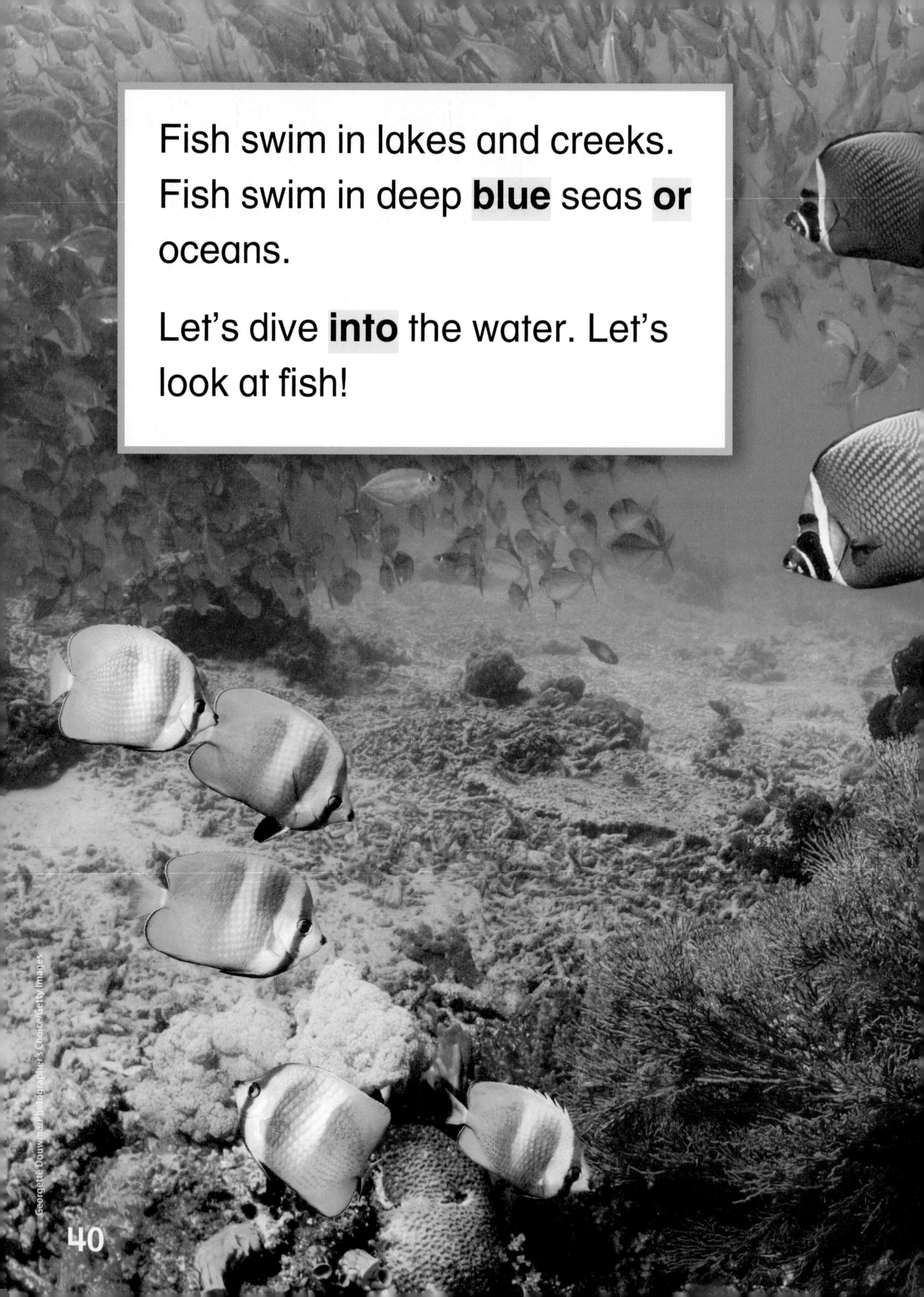

Fish can swim alone. Fish can swim with a **partner**.

Fish can swim in a bunch, too. A bunch of fish is called a school.

A school has lots of fish.
They are a team.

The fish help each **other**. They look for food together.

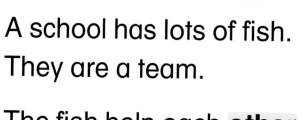

Reinhard Dirscherl/Alamy

Fish eat lots of things. Some fish eat **small** animals. Some fish eat other fish!

These catfish eat together for safety.

It can be unsafe to swim alone.
What is the chief reason? **Danger!**
A fish can get snapped up!

But a fish can hide in a school.

Georgette Douwma/Photographer's Choice/Getty Images

Fish in a school have a neat trick. The fish swim close together.

Big fish will not mess with them **because** they look like one huge fish.

These crescent-tail bigeye fish swim in a school to fool big fish.

(inset) Fred Bavendam/Minden Pictures

This big fish wants to eat. But it stays away. The school looks like a huge fish that may eat him!

Georgette Douwma/Photographer's Choice/Getty Images

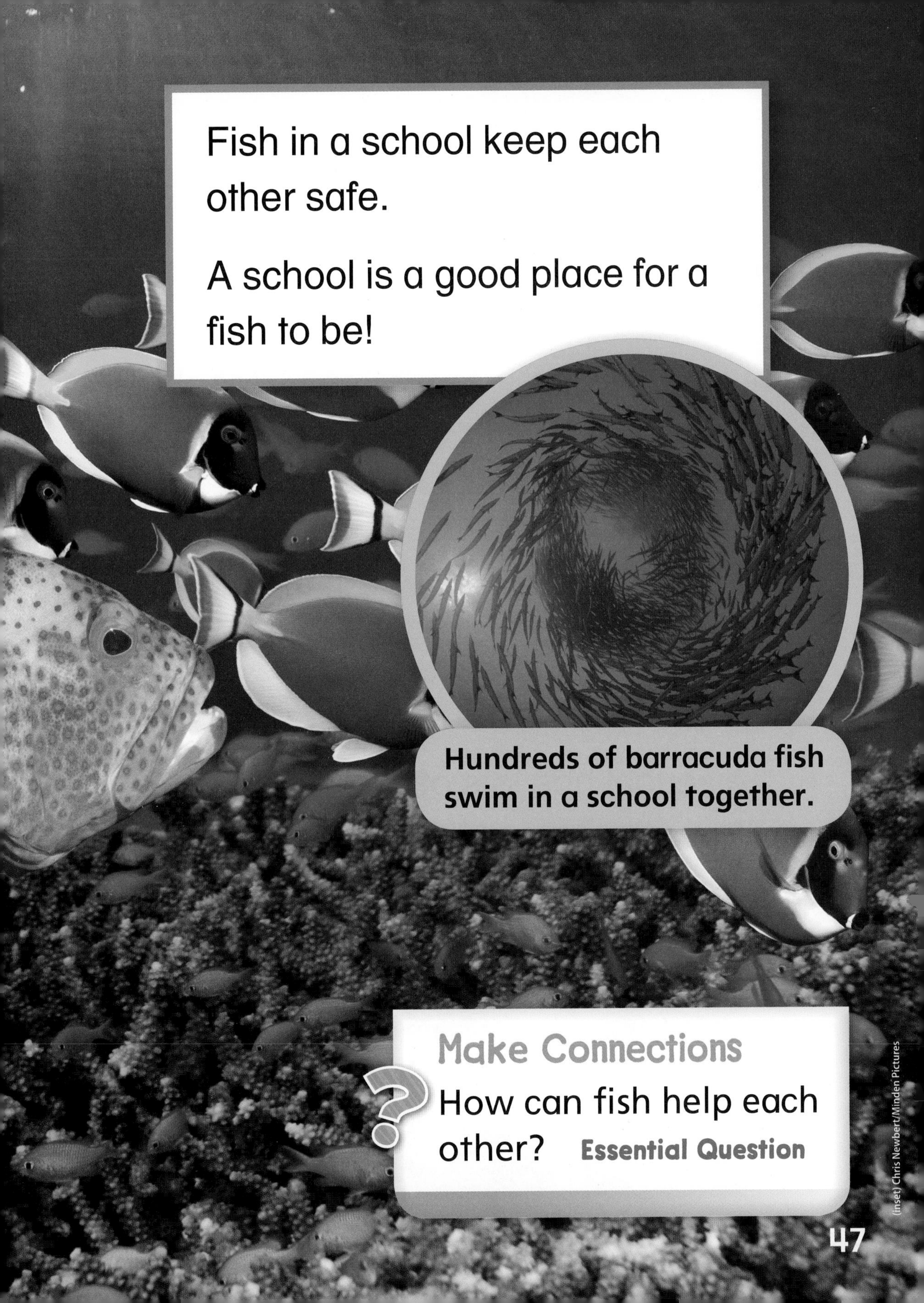

Fish in a school keep each other safe.

A school is a good place for a fish to be!

Hundreds of barracuda fish swim in a school together.

Make Connections

How can fish help each other? **Essential Question**

Main Idea and Key Details

The **main idea** is what the selection is mostly about.

Key details give information about the main idea.

Find Text Evidence

Find a detail about how fish in a school help each other.

page 42

A school has lots of fish.
They are a team.

The fish help each **other**. They look for food together.

Reinhard Dirscherl/Alamy

Read Together

Main Idea

Fish in a school help each other.

Detail

The fish look for food together.

Detail

The fish keep each other safe.

Detail

They help keep big fish away.

Your Turn

Talk about the main idea and details in "A Team of Fish."

Go Digital! *Use the interactive graphic organizer*

CCSS **Writing and Grammar**

Readers to...

Organization Lee introduced the topic of his report first.

Lee's Report

Ants work as a team. Each ant has a job. The queen lays eggs. Other ants get food. Ants have many ways to get their jobs done.

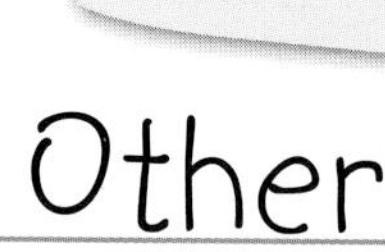

Your Turn

Tell how Lee organized his report.

Read Together

Writers

Have and Has Use **has** to tell about one person or thing. Use **have** to tell about more than one person or thing.

Each ant **has** a job.
Ants **have** many ways to get their jobs done.

COLLABORATE

Your Turn

- Look at the sentences above from Lee's report. Do they tell about one or more than one?
- Write a new sentence with **has**. Write a new sentence with **have**.

Mike Dammer

Weekly Concept In the Wild

Essential Question

How do animals survive in nature?

Go Digital!

Inaki Relanzon/naturepl.com

Survivors!

COLLABORATE

Talk About It

How does this eagle get food to eat?

find

Fish can **find** a place to hide.

food

All animals need **food** to live.

more

We give it **more** food to eat.

over

The girl jumps **over** the rope.

start

When does a cub **start** to walk?

warm

The lion sat in the **warm** sun.

search

Do bees **search** for plants?

seek

A bear will **seek** out ripe berries.

COLLABORATE

Your Turn

Read the sentence for each word. Then make up another sentence.

Go Digital! *Use the online visual glossary*

(t to b, l to r) Brand X Pictures/PunchStock; Organics image library/Alamy; Image Source/Getty Images; ImageDJ/Alamy; imagebroker.net/SuperStock; Paul Allen/Robert Harding World Imagery/Getty Images; Creatas Images/PictureQuest/Getty Images; altrendo nature/Stockbyte/Getty Images

Long o

The letters o, oa, ow, and oe make the long o sound in **go**, **road**, **crow**, and **doe**.

old	**boats**	**showing**
Joe	**most**	**groan**
slow	**toes**	**told**
goes	**toasted**	**window**

Read Together

Joe used soap to clean the bowl.

He soaked it in cold water.

Your Turn

COLLABORATE

Look for these words with long o in "Go Wild!"

go	**grow**	**don't**
hippos	**hippo**	**loads**
snow	**toads**	**goes**
no	**so**	**both**
cold	**most**	

CCSS **Genre** Nonfiction

Essential Question

How do animals survive in nature?

Read about how animals in the wild find food.

Go Digital!

EckPhoto/Alamy

GO WiLD!

Animals need **food** to live and grow. But all animals don't eat the same things. Some big animals such as hippos eat plants. A hippo can eat **more** than 130 pounds of grass!

Kennan Ward/Corbis

Some small animals eat plants, too. A squirrel eats loads of plant seeds. They like nuts and grains. A squirrel can smell a nut and **find** it even in the snow!

Alex Fieldhouse/Alamy

Some animals hunt and eat other animals. First this big cat runs fast to catch its meal. Then it will use its claws and teeth to eat.

Andy Rouse/The Image Bank/Getty Images

Frogs and toads **seek** insects and snails to eat. A big frog goes after mice, too. But frogs and toads have no teeth. So they must gulp down their meal!

craftvision/Vetta/Getty Images

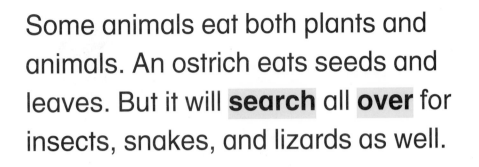

Some animals eat both plants and animals. An ostrich eats seeds and leaves. But it will **search** all **over** for insects, snakes, and lizards as well.

Carl & Ann Purcell/Corbis

A painted turtle eats plants, fish, and frogs. This reptile lives in lakes and ponds. It likes the cold water at first. But then it will come up on land to get **warm**.

Andrew McLachlan/All Canada Photos/Getty Images

A bear may **start** its day by eating plants. Next, it may go fishing in a lake. After that, a bear may go hunting. Then, it may even go to a campsite.

Andy Rouse/The Image Bank/Getty Images

Most bears will eat plants, animals, and people food. Is there any food left here to eat? If so, a bear will find it! In the wild, animals find food in lots of places.

Make Connections

What do animals in the wild eat? **Essential Question**

Juniors Bildarchiv/Alamy

Main Idea and Key Details

The **main idea** is what the selection is mostly about.

Key details give information about the main idea.

Find Text Evidence

Find key details about what animals in the wild eat.

page 60

Animals need **food** to live and grow. But all animals don't eat the same things. Some big animals such as hippos eat plants. A hippo can eat **more** than 130 pounds of grass!

Kennan Ward/Corbis

Read Together

Main Idea

Animals in the wild eat many different things.

Detail	Detail	Detail
Some animals such as hippos eat plants.	Some animals such as ostriches eat both plants and animals.	Some animals such as frogs eat other animals.

COLLABORATE

Your Turn

Talk about the main idea and details in "Go Wild!"

Go Digital! *Use the interactive graphic organizer*

Corbis Flirt/Alamy

Readers to...

Organization Joe wrote a concluding sentence at the end of his sea gulls report.

Joe's Report

Do sea gulls eat plants?
I saw one at the beach that did.
Sea gulls go after fish.
One I saw even went after bugs.
Sea gulls eat almost anything.

Your Turn

COLLABORATE

Tell how Joe organized the end of his report.

Read Together

Writers

Go and Do The action words **go** and **do** tell about now. The action words **went** and **did** tell about the past.

Do sea gulls eat plants?

Sea gulls **go** after fish.

COLLABORATE

Your Turn

- Find sentences with **went** and **did** in Joe's report.
- Write new sentences with **go, went, do,** and **did**.

Candace Trew Camling

Weekly Concept Insects!

Essential Question

What insects do you know about? How are they alike and different?

Go Digital!

altrendo nature/Altrendo/Getty Images

Bug Me!

Talk About It

What is special about the caterpillar? How is it like other bugs?

Words to Know

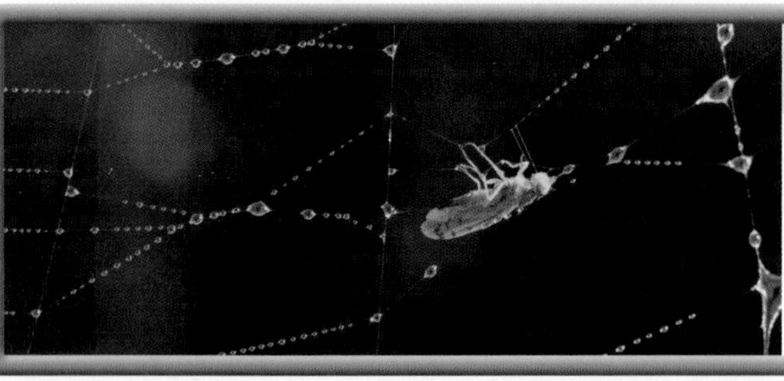

caught

A bug is **caught** in this web.

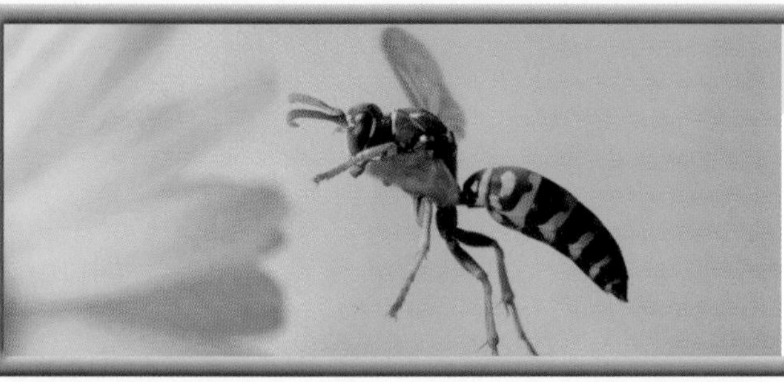

flew

The wasp **flew** over to the flower.

know

I **know** how to catch a bug!

laugh

That bug story made us **laugh**.

listen

Listen to the buzzing bees!

were

Fireflies **were** out last night.

beautiful

The butterfly has **beautiful** wings.

fancy

We are wearing **fancy** hats.

COLLABORATE

Your Turn

Read the sentence for each word. Then make up another sentence.

Go Digital! *Use the online visual glossary*

Long i

The letters i, y, igh, and ie make the long i sound in **find**, **fly**, **high**, and **cries**.

by	**untie**	**sighed**
mild	**sky**	**tries**
dry	**kind**	**relight**
right	**child**	**spied**

Daniel Moreton

Dwight spied a moth by the light.

"What kind is it?" I asked myself.

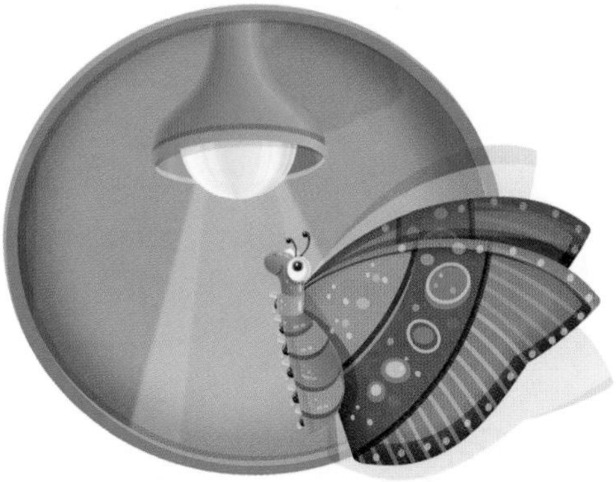

Your Turn

COLLABORATE

Look for these words with long i in "Creep Low, Fly High."

fly	**high**	**I**	**sighed**
cried	**right**	**find**	**sky**
by	**hi**	**I'm**	

CCSS **Genre** Fantasy

Essential Question

What insects do you know about? How are they alike and different?

Read about what some insects are like.

Go Digital!

Creep Low, Fly High

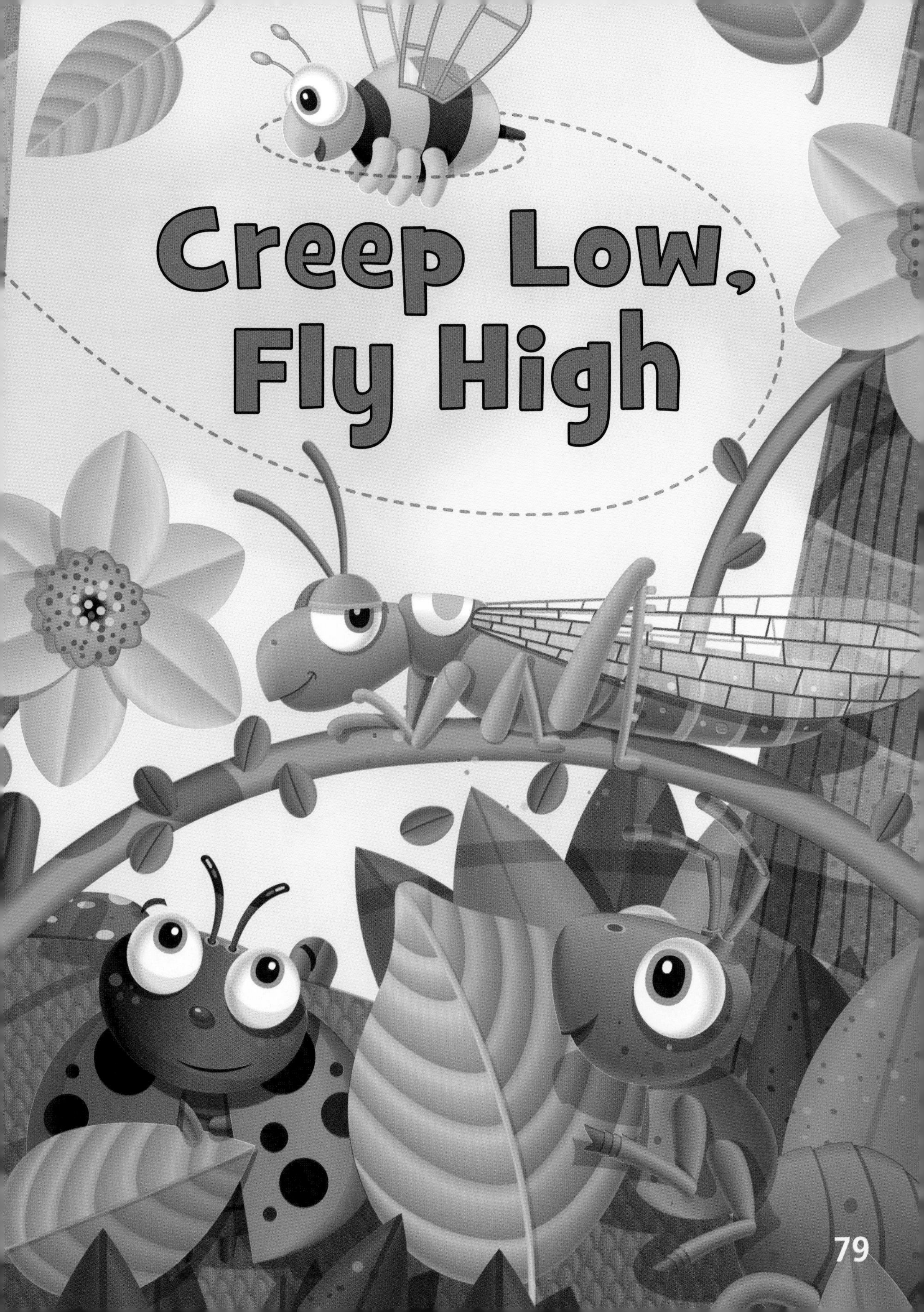

Bug Boasts

The sun came up over a big field.
Five bug pals met to chat and **laugh**.

Grasshopper boasted a bit. "I can hop to the top of any plant!"

Daniel Moreton

"Well, I can dash fast," bragged Ant.

"**Listen**!" hummed Bee. "I can buzz as I fly high."

"And I can zip around on **fancy** spotted wings!" smiled Ladybug.

"Not I," sighed Caterpillar.
"I just creep, creep, creep."
Then he crept away.

"Come back!" his pals wailed.
But Caterpillar did not.

Missing!

It was time for lunch. The bugs did not see Caterpillar. He was missing! Where did he go?

"I think I **know** where he is!" cried Ant. "He is hiding because he feels bad."

"I think that's right," nodded Grasshopper. "Let's find him. We can cheer him up!"

The two rushed away.

"What if he is not hiding?" asked Bee. "I saw a bird when we **were** chatting,"added Bee. "It **flew** low in the sky."

"What if it **caught** our pal?" cried Ladybug. "We must find out! Maybe we can save him!"

The two flew away.

Still a Pal

The bugs did not find Caterpillar. Many days went by. The pals were sad. Then one day they saw a **beautiful** bug with gold wings.

"Hi! I'm back!" the bug called as he flew by. "I wrapped up and rested. Then I popped out like this!"

Daniel Moreton

"It's me—Butterfly! I used to be Caterpillar!" cried Butterfly.

"But you are not the same," sighed Ant.

"But I am still a pal," said Butterfly. "And now I can flit and dip! Let's go have some fun!"

Make Connections

How can insects be alike and different?

Essential Question

Point of View

Point of view is the way that a story character thinks or feels.

Find Text Evidence

Find the point of view of one of the story characters.

page 84

"I think I **know** where he is!" cried Ant. "He is hiding because he feels bad."

Daniel Moreton

Read Together

Character	Clue	Point of View
Ant	Thinks that Caterpillar is hiding because he feels bad.	Is worried about Caterpillar.
Ladybug	Thinks that a bird caught Caterpillar.	Wants to save Caterpillar.
Caterpillar/ Butterfly	Tells Ant that he can now flit and dip.	Is happy to be a butterfly who can fly!

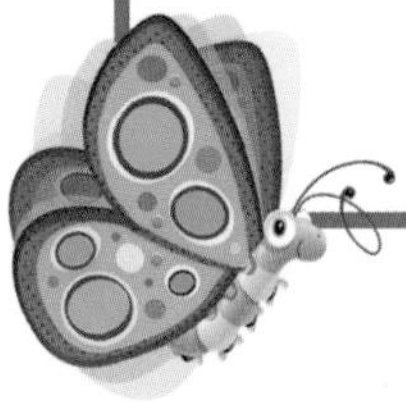

COLLABORATE

Your Turn

Talk about the different points of view in "Creep Low, Fly High."

Go Digital! *Use the interactive graphic organizer*

Readers to...

Organization Sky wrote a strong ending for her book review.

Sky's Book Review

I liked reading "Bugs at Night."
I saw cute bugs in the story.
I saw what they did at night.
The bugs see a bat and hide.
You must read this good story!

Your Turn

COLLABORATE

Tell how Sky organized her writing.

Read Together

Writers

See and Saw Some verbs change spelling when they tell about the past. **See** and **sees** tell about the present. **Saw** tells about the past.

I **saw** cute bugs in the story.
The bugs **see** a bat
and hide.

Your Turn

- Find another sentence that uses **see** or **saw**. Does it tell about the present or the past?
- Write new sentences with **see** or **saw**.

CCSS Weekly Concept Working with Animals

Essential Question

How do people work with animals?

Go Digital!

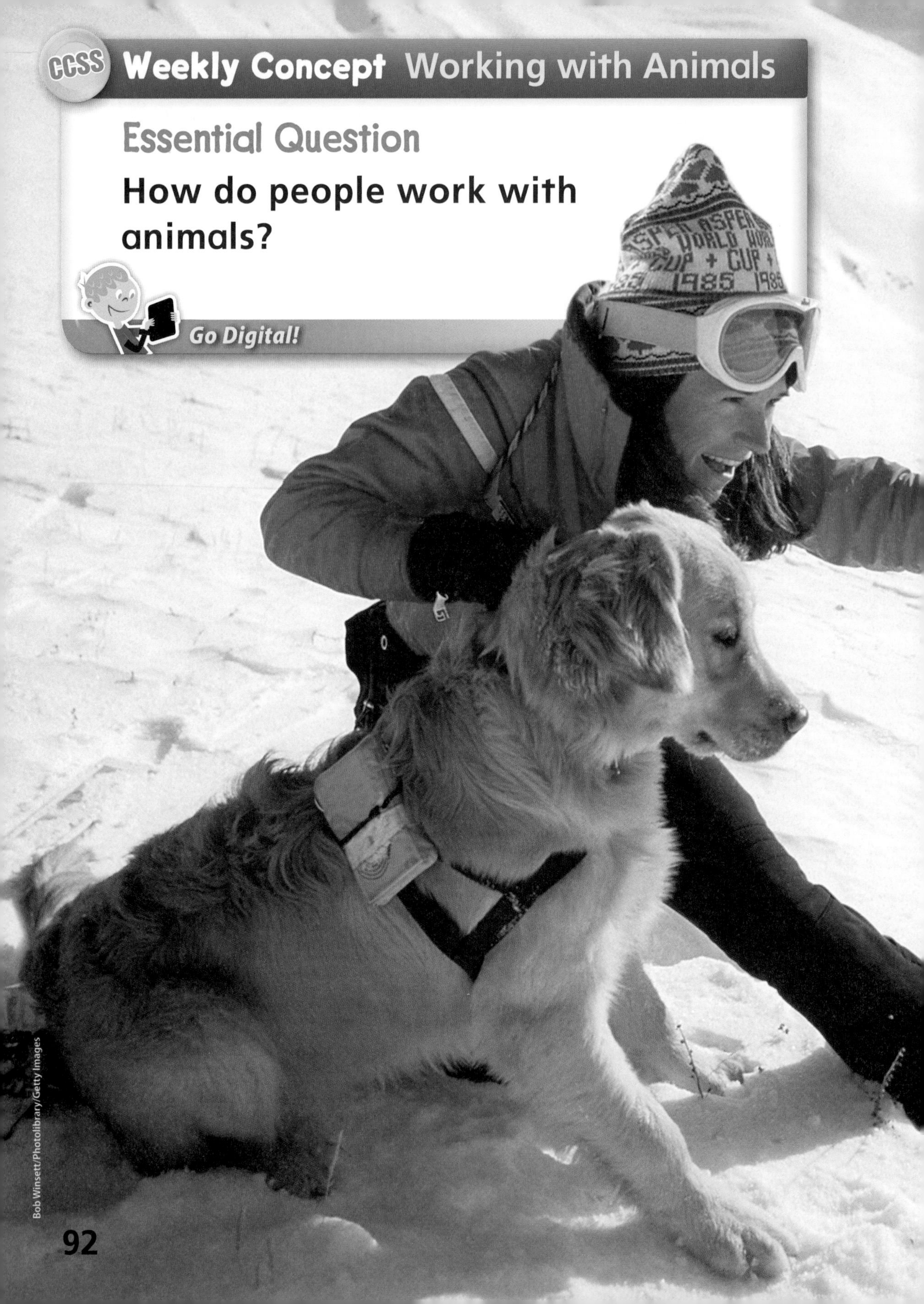

Bob Winsett/Photolibrary/Getty Images

TIME FOR KIDS®

Animals and Us

Talk About It

What is the trainer teaching this dog?

CCSS Words to Know

found

The dog **found** a bone.

hard

The horses are working **hard**.

near

The dog is **near** the trainer.

woman

The **woman** walks the dog.

would

She **would** like to ride.

Read Together

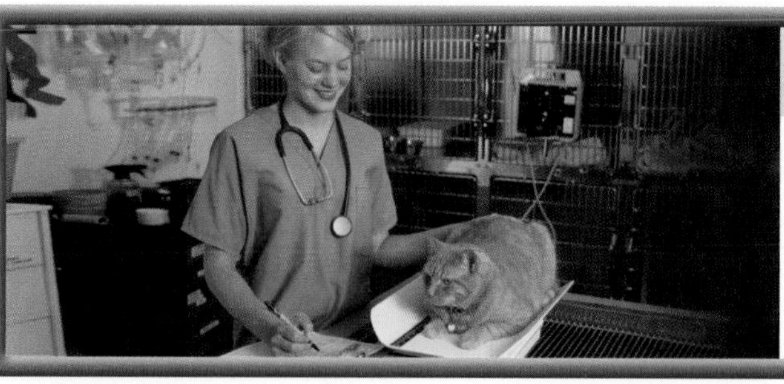

write

She will **write** what we need.

clever

This bird is very **clever**!

signal

The trainer gives a **signal**.

COLLABORATE

Your Turn

Read the sentence for each word. Then make up another sentence.

Go Digital! *Use the online visual glossary*

(t to b, l to r) Peter Titmuss/Alamy; Jim Parkin/Alamy; Jim Craigmyle/Corbis; John W. Banagan/Photographer's Choice/Getty Images; Paul Mansfield/Flickr/Getty Images; Corbis/PunchStock; Tracey Charleson/Photo Researchers/Getty Images; Minden Pictures/SuperStock

Long e

The letters y and ey can make the long e sound in **puppy** and **key**.

lucky	**alley**	**sunny**
buddy	**Mickey**	**city**
easy	**penny**	**sleepy**
grassy	**valley**	**healthy**

Paul Eric Rosa

Read Together

Did you lose your key in the alley?

We walk Ziggy when it is sunny.

Your Turn

COLLABORATE

Look for these words with long e in "From Puppy to Guide Dog."

puppy	**key**	**Mickey**	**buddy**
lazy	**fussy**	**healthy**	**city**
ready	**easy**		

CCSS **Genre** Nonfiction

TIME FOR KIDS®

Essential Question

How do people work with animals?

Read about how people train guide dogs.

Go Digital!

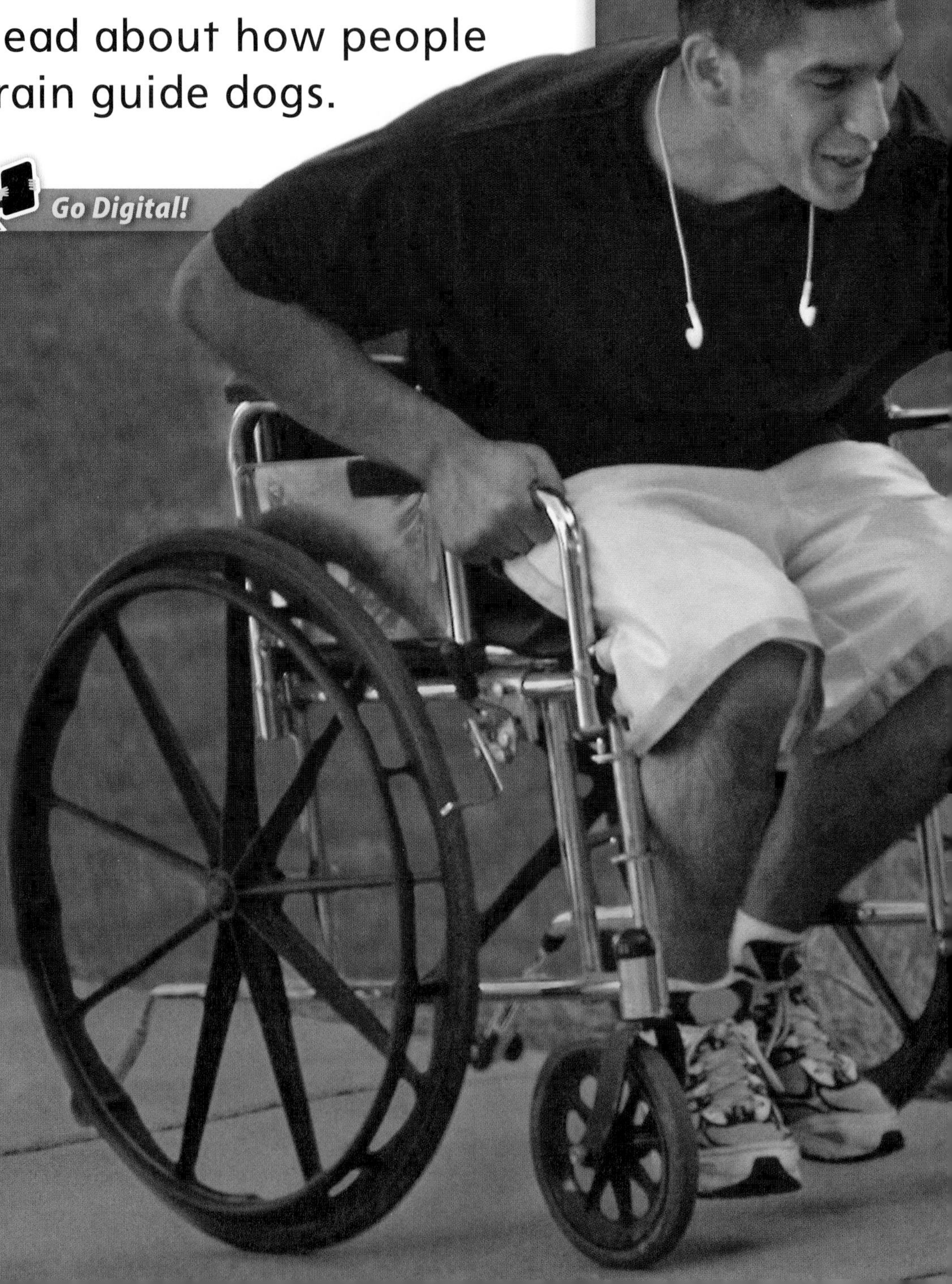

Frederic Larson/San Francisco Chronicle/Corbis

From Puppy to Guide Dog

Most dogs are pets. But some dogs help people. What is the key to making a dog a good helping dog?

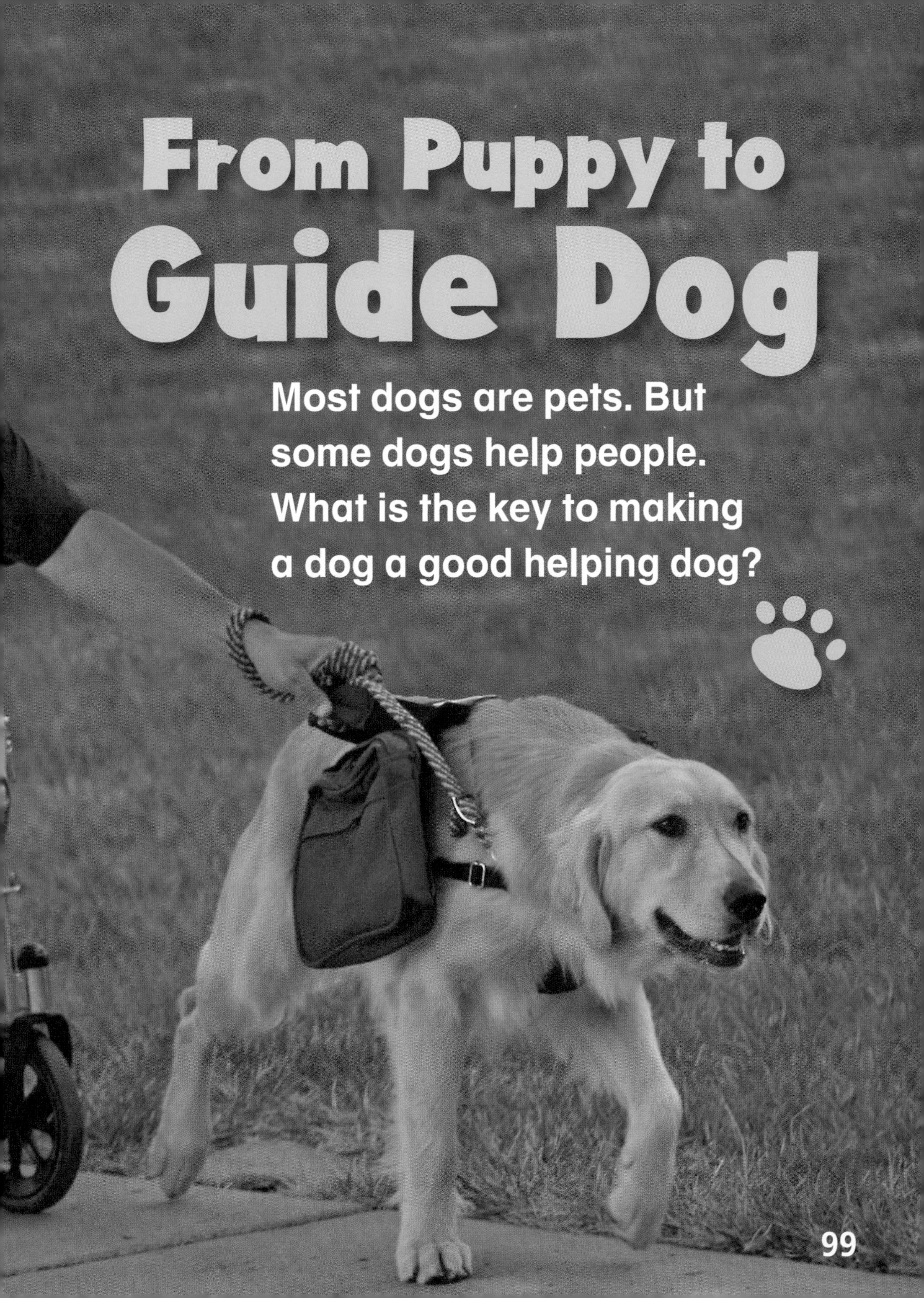

A Buddy-to-Be

Mickey is a cute and **clever** puppy. He runs, jumps, and plays. One day, when he grows up a bit, Mickey will be a helping dog. He will be a daily buddy to a person who cannot see.

(l) Juniors Bildarchiv/age fotostock; (r) Getty Images/Photodisc

Helping dogs are called guide dogs. To be a guide dog, a puppy must be bright. It cannot be lazy or fussy. The puppy will need to learn many skills. A new home is **found** for the puppy when it is eight weeks old.

Fact

Most guide dogs are Labrador retrievers. They are very intelligent and easy to train.

▼ Guide dogs can be big or tiny.

Ryan McVay/Photolibrary

A Family of Trainers

A puppy like Mickey stays with a family for at least one year. The family plays with it and feeds it. They help the puppy stay healthy and teach the puppy a lot.

Jim Craigmyle/Comet/Corbis

▲ Each puppy has checkups at the vet.

Fact

10,000 people in the U.S. and Canada use guide dogs.

Each puppy learns how to act nicely with people and with other animals. The family gets the dog used to a lot of tasks and settings. Puppies may visit many kinds of places in the city. They go to homes and shops.

▲ This dog watches its favorite team.

▼ Every dog must be trained by itself.

(t) Tom & Dee Ann McCarthy/Bridge/Corbis; (b) PA/Topham/The Image Works

Learning New Tasks

As time goes by, the dogs are trained how to go across the street. The dog stays right **near** the trainer. It learns to stop at a red **signal**. This will help the dog safely lead a person who cannot see the traffic.

Fact

Guide dogs are allowed in restaurants, stores, school—any place a person can go.

Zuma Press/Newscom

▲ This guide dog learns to cross a street.

Some guide dogs can be trained to help a man or a **woman** who cannot move or walk. He or she might need help with a lot of **hard** tasks both inside and outside the home.

A dog can be trained to get an elevator and to reach objects.

Eyes and Ears

Some dogs are trained to help people who cannot hear. If the dog hears a bell ringing or a yell, it **would** lightly tug or poke the person with its nose.

A dog can be taught to alert its owner to sounds.

Fact

Guide dogs should not be bothered while working.

Yan Sheng/CNImaging/Newscom

Ready to Guide

Training a puppy for a year is not an easy job. Owners may call or **write** to thank the family that raised their puppy.

Training a guide dog helps a lot of people!

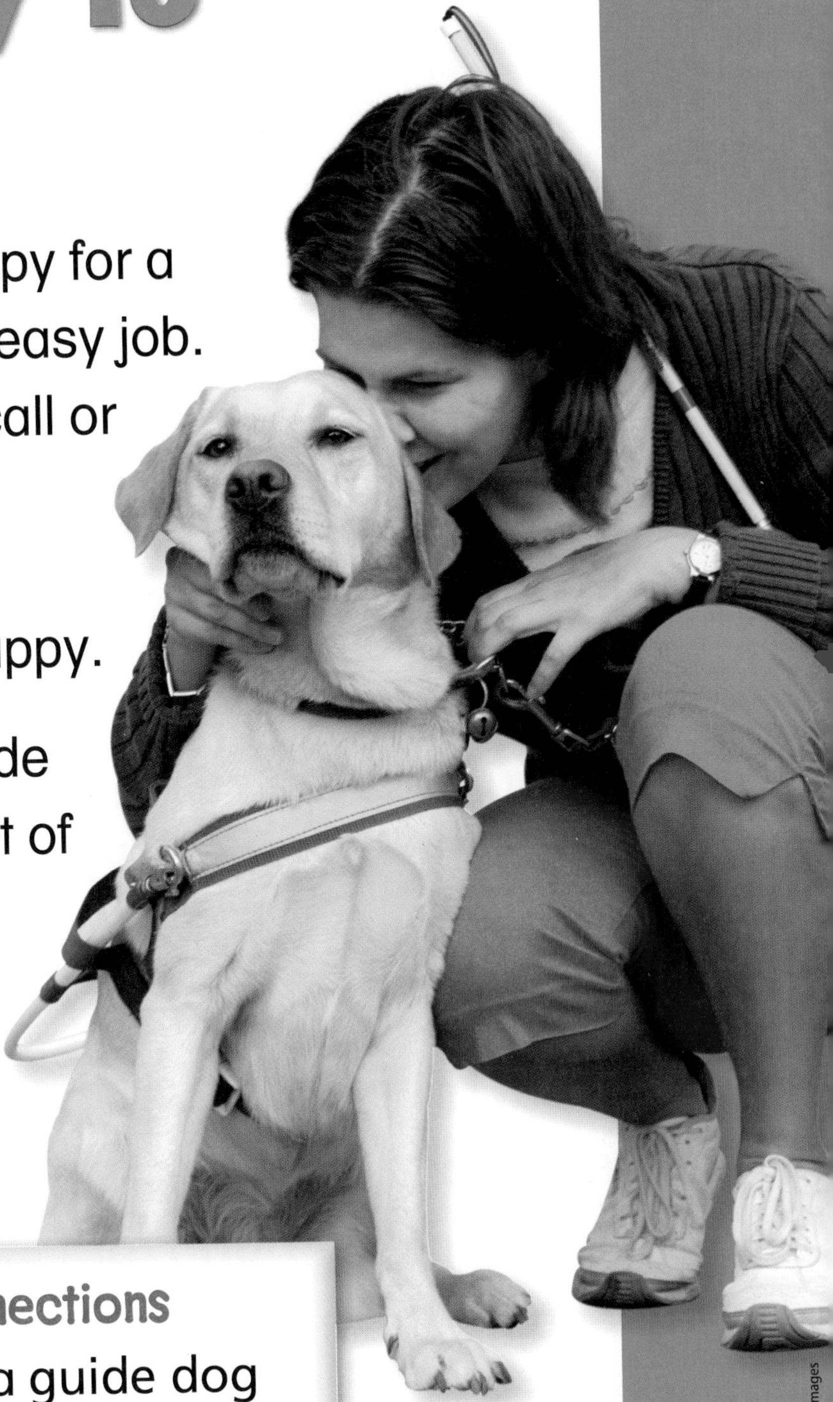

Altrendo Images/Getty Images

Make Connections

How does a guide dog get trained to help people? **Essential Question**

Sequence

Authors often give information in **sequence**, or time order.

Find Text Evidence

Find one of the first things that happens to a guide dog puppy.

page 101

Helping dogs are called guide dogs. To be a guide dog, a puppy must be bright. It cannot be lazy or fussy. The puppy will need to learn many skills. A new home is **found** for the puppy when it is eight weeks old.

Read Together

First

An eight-week-old puppy leaves its mother.

Next

It lives with a training family for one year.

Then

The puppy learns harder tasks. It becomes a good guide dog.

Last

The guide dog is given to a needy person.

Your Turn

Talk about the sequence of a guide dog's life in "From Puppy to Guide Dog."

Go Digital! *Use the interactive graphic organizer*

Readers to...

Word Choice Jenny used words that tell time order in her sentences.

Jenny's How-to Sentences

How can you care for a dog? First, give it food and water. Next, walk with it. Then, play fetch. Later, give it a treat. The dog will be happy!

Your Turn

COLLABORATE

Tell what words Jenny used to tell time order.

Writers

Adverbs That Tell When Words such as **first, always, next, later, tomorrow, soon, early, today, then**, and **yesterday** tell when an action takes place.

First, give it food
and water.

COLLABORATE

Your Turn

- Find other words in Jenny's writing that tell when an action takes place.
- Write new sentences using words that tell when.

Paul Eric Rosa

Unit 5

Figure It Out

The Big Idea

How can we make sense of the world around us?

My Shadow

I have a little shadow that
goes in and out with me,

And what can be the use of
him is more than I can see.

He is very, very like me from
the heels up to the head;

And I see him jump before me,
when I jump into my bed.

—by Robert Louis Stevenson

Weekly Concept See It, Sort It

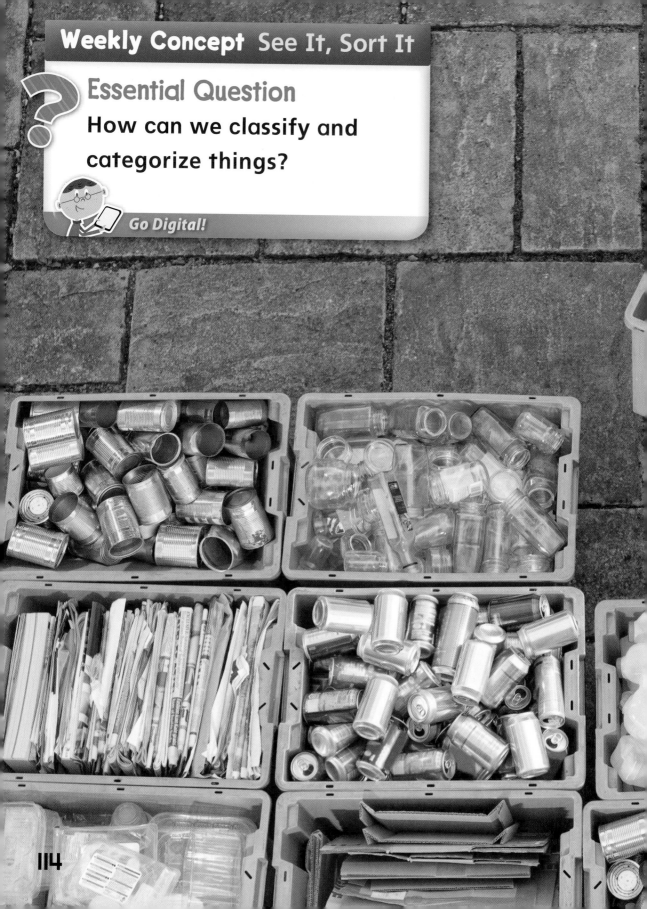

Essential Question

How can we classify and categorize things?

Go Digital!

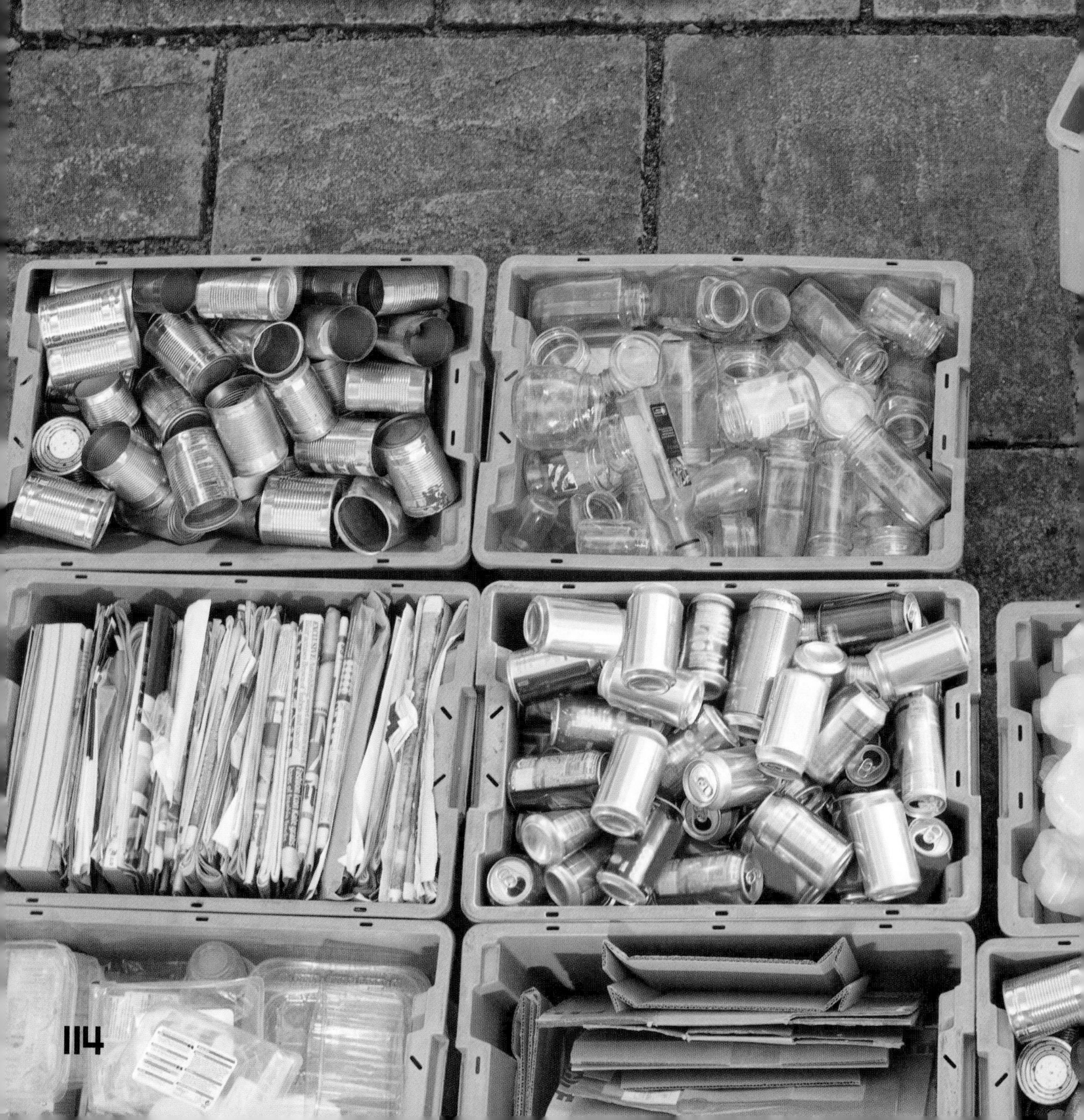

Les & Dave Jacobs/Cultura/Getty Images

Mix and Match

COLLABORATE

Talk About It

How is this girl sorting things?

CCSS Words to Know

four

A sheep has **four** legs.

large

We picked a **large** pumpkin.

none

None of the dogs has spots.

only

This goat has **only** one kid.

put

We **put** the best peaches in the box.

round

A tractor has big **round** wheels.

trouble

A goat can get into **trouble**!

whole

The **whole** barn is painted red.

Your Turn

Read the sentence for each word. Then make up another sentence.

Go Digital! *Use the online visual glossary*

(t to b, l to r) Photo 24/Brand X Pictures/Getty Images; Digital Vision; Photodisc Collection/Getty Images; NaturePL/SuperStock; Daniel Hurst Photography/ Photographer's Choice/Getty Images; age fotostock/SuperStock; Frank Naylor/Alamy; Steve Hamblin/Alamy

ar

The letters ar can make the sounds you hear in the middle of **barn**.

part	farm	park
large	marching	smart
sharp	hard	started
restart	backyard	artist

Jack Hughes

Read Together

Marge has a large farm with a red barn.

She parks her car in the yard.

COLLABORATE

Your Turn

Look for these words with ar in "A Barn Full of Hats."

barn	**farm**	**smart**
marched	**yarn**	**apart**
Clark	**large**	**barnyard**

CCSS **Genre** Fantasy

Essential Question

How can we classify and categorize things?

Read about how some farm animals sort hats.

Go Digital!

Jack Hughes

A Barn Full of Hats

One day, **four** farm animals found a box in the barn. They opened it up.

What was inside? Hats, hats, and more hats!

Jack Hughes

"Look at all those hats! Who wants one?" asked Hen.

"I do!" cried Horse. "It's smart to wear a hat. A hat will keep the sun out of my eyes."

Hen stuck her head in the box. She pulled out a flat, **round** hat. "Try this hat," Hen told Horse.

"No, that hat is too flat," said Horse.

"A flat hat makes a good nest!" clucked Hen. So she took the hat and she marched away.

Jack Hughes

Pig pushed his head in the box. He pulled out a bright red hat. "**Put** on this hat," Pig told Horse.

"No, that hat is too red," said Horse.

"A red hat looks fine!" grunted Pig. So he put on the hat and he marched away.

Cat poked her head in the box.
She pulled out a thick yarn hat.
"Try this hat!" Cat told Horse.

"No, that hat is too thick," said Horse.

Jack Hughes

"Thick yarn is nice," said Cat. "I will take the **whole** hat apart, so I can play with the yarn." She dragged the hat away.

"So many hats, but **none** for me!" sighed Horse.

Just then, Farmer Clark came into the barn. His hat was **large** and floppy.

"If **only** I had that hat!" said Horse. "That hat will shade my eyes!"

Horse grabbed the hat in his teeth!

Jack Hughes

Farmer Clark laughed. He put the hat on Horse. It stayed on with no **trouble**. "It fits well," Farmer Clark said.

Horse trotted to the barnyard. Clip, clop! He held his head high. "Yes, this is the hat for me!" said Horse.

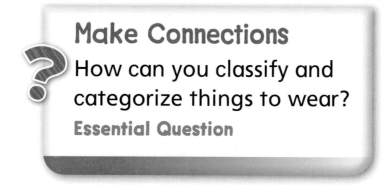

Make Connections

How can you classify and categorize things to wear?

Essential Question

Point of View

Point of view is the way that a story character thinks or feels.

What a character says helps you understand his or her point of view.

Find Text Evidence

Find the point of view of one of the story characters.

page 123

"Look at all those hats! Who wants one?" asked Hen.

"I do!" cried Horse. "It's smart to wear a hat. A hat will keep the sun out of my eyes."

Jack Hughes

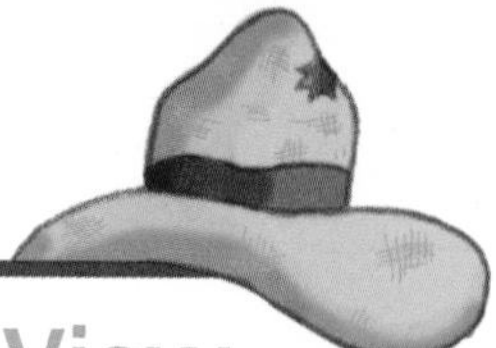

Character	Clue	Point of View
Horse	Thinks it's smart to wear a hat.	Wants something to shade his eyes from the sun.
Hen	Takes the hat to use as a nest.	Wants to find good materials for her nest.
Cat	Likes the hat made of thick yarn.	Wants something to play with.

Your Turn

COLLABORATE

Talk about the different points of view in "A Barn Full of Hats."

Go Digital! *Use the interactive graphic organizer*

Readers to...

Sentence Fluency Mark used complete sentences in his directions.

Mark's Directions to Farmer Clark's Field

Start at the barn and walk to the big fence. Then open the gate so you can go in the field. The field is past the tree.

Your Turn

- Tell how you know Mark's sentences are complete.
- Tell what you will write directions to.

Read Together

Writers

Words That Join You can use **and, but, or, so,** and **because** to join sentences.

Start at the barn
and walk to the
big fence.

Your Turn

COLLABORATE

- Find another place in Mark's directions where he joined two sentences.
- Write two new sentences. Join them using **and, but, or, so,** or **because**.

Jack Hughes

Weekly Concept Up in the Sky

Essential Question

What can you see in the sky?

Go Digital!

Talk About It

COLLABORATE

What does this girl see in the night sky?

(bkgd) StockTrek/Getty Images; Image Source/Getty Images

Night and Day

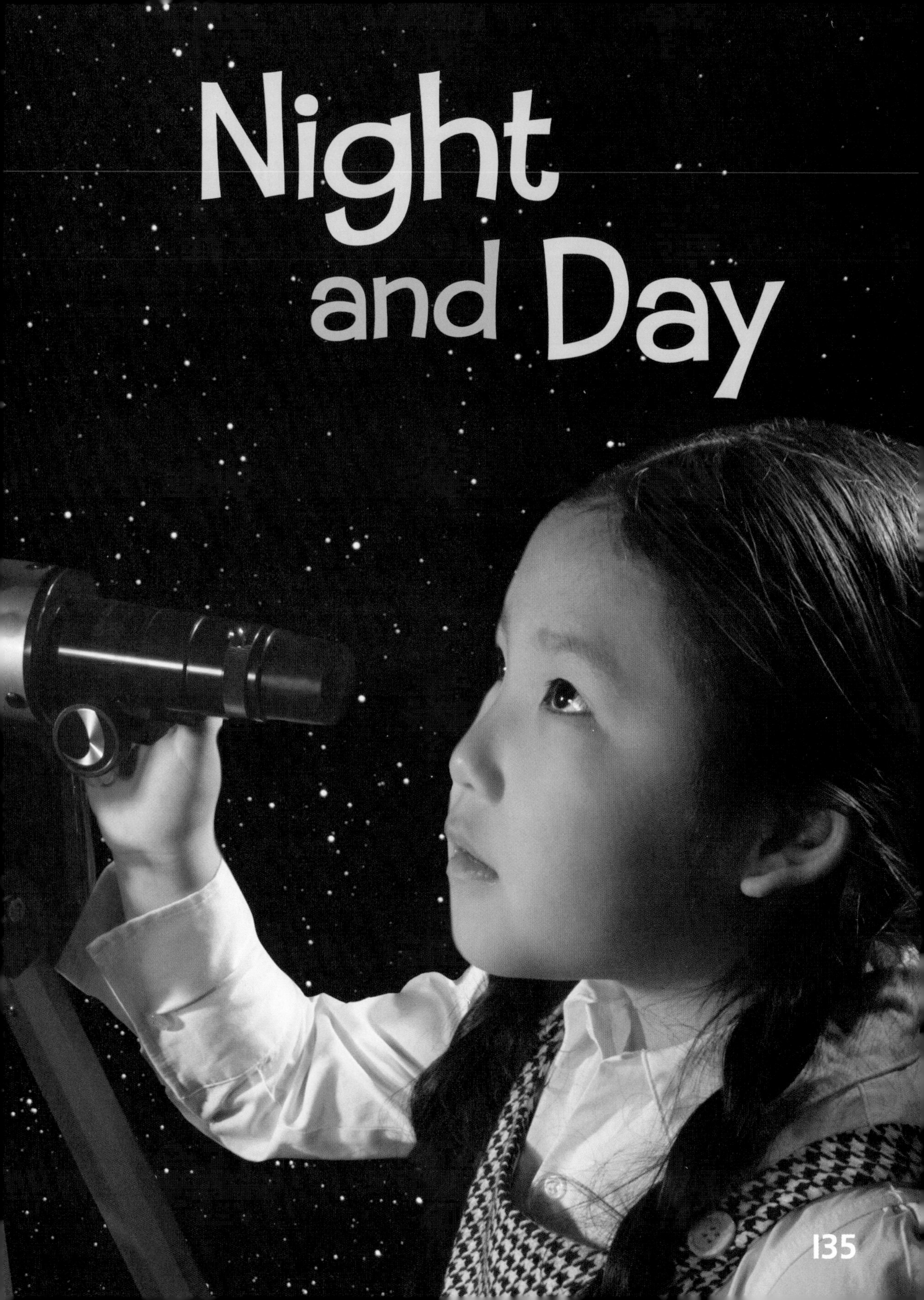

CCSS Words to Know

another

Will **another** cloud cover the sun?

climb

That cat can **climb** a tree quickly.

full

There is a **full** moon out tonight.

great

It is a **great** day for a picnic!

poor

My **poor** dog got wet in the rain.

Read Together

through

Can you see the man **through** the fog?

leaped

The frog **leaped** into the lake.

stretched

The rainbow **stretched** out across the sky.

Your Turn

Read the sentence for each word. Then make up another sentence.

Go Digital! *Use the online visual glossary*

er, ir, ur, or

The letters er, ir, ur, and or can make the sounds you hear in the middle of **term**, **bird**, **curl**, and **worm**.

girl	**dirt**	**hurt**
her	**worked**	**third**
turns	**verb**	**first**
shirt	**word**	**nurse**

Lisa Hunt

Read Together

Did that burst of thunder wake Herb?

Herb woke up first and turned over.

Your Turn

COLLABORATE

Look for these words with er, ir, ur, and or in "A Bird Named Fern."

bird	**Fern**	**world**
herself	**her**	**surprised**
better	**turned**	**first**

CCSS **Genre** Fantasy

Essential Question

What can you see in the sky?

Read how a bird named Fern learns about clouds.

Go Digital!

Lisa Hunt

A Bird Named Fern

Little Fern was always **full** of questions! She wanted to know about everything in the world.

Lisa Hunt

One day, Fern saw something up in the sky.

"What is that big, white boat doing in the sky?" she asked herself. "I want to find out."

"It would be **great** to ride on that big white boat," Fern said. So she **stretched** her wings and took off.

Lisa Hunt

Fern's wings helped her **climb** up, up, up.

But when she got close to the boat, she was surprised. The boat looked like a fluffy bed!

Fern was sleepy and wanted to rest. So she **leaped** on the bed. But she fell right **through** it!

Lisa Hunt

"I see **another** bed," said Fern. "I will try to land on that one."

But the same thing happened again!

"I'd better go home," cried Fern. "Maybe Mom and Dad can explain this."

So Fern began to fly home. As she did, the beds turned dark gray. Then it started to rain. **Poor** Fern was soaked when she got home.

"Where were you?" asked Mom and Dad.

Fern told them all about her trip.

"First we will dry you off," said Mom.

"Then we will teach you about clouds," added Dad.

And that is what they did!

Lisa Hunt

Make Connections

What did the clouds look like to Fern? **Essential Question**

Cause and Effect

A **cause** is what makes something happen in a story.

An **effect** is the event that happens.

To figure out cause and effect, ask yourself: What happened? Why did it happen?

Find Text Evidence

Find a cause and its effect in the story.

page 144

"It would be **great** to ride on that big white boat," Fern said. So she **stretched** her wings and took off.

Lisa Hunt

Read Together

Cause	Effect
Fern wanted to ride on the big white boat.	Fern stretched her wings and took off.
The boat looked like a fluffy bed up close.	Fern was surprised.
It started to rain.	Fern got soaked.

Your Turn

Talk about the cause and effect of story events in "A Bird Named Fern."

Go Digital! *Use the interactive graphic organizer*

Readers to...

Word Choice Albert wrote a description of a place. He used many adjectives.

Albert's Description

It was a hot day. I found a big cave. It was dark and quiet inside. I was surprised to see a soft red mat.

Your Turn

- Tell what adjectives Albert used in his description.
- Tell what adjectives you will use in your description.

Read Together

Writers

Adjectives are words that describe. They may describe size, shape, number, and color. They may tell how things look, sound, feel, smell, and taste.

I found a **big** cave.
It was **dark** and
quiet inside.

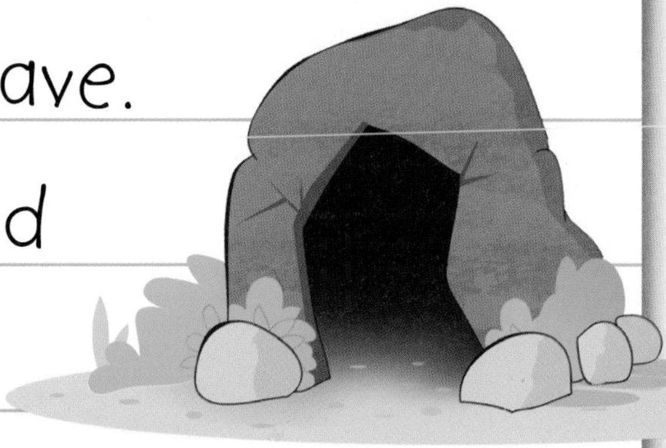

COLLABORATE

Your Turn

- Find more adjectives in Albert's description.
- Write new sentences with adjectives. Circle the adjectives in each sentence.

Lisa Hunt

Weekly Concept Great Inventions

Essential Question

What inventions do you know about?

Go Digital!

Talk About It

How do you use this invention?

SuperStock

A New Idea

CCSS

Words to Know

began

He **began** to build a robot.

better

Let's invent a **better** umbrella!

guess

Can you **guess** what this does?

learn

You can **learn** how to sign just like me!

right

This clock tells the **right** time.

Read Together

sure

She makes **sure** you are well.

idea

New bulbs are a good **idea**!

unusual

This new bike is **unusual**.

COLLABORATE

Your Turn

Read the sentence for each word. Then make up another sentence.

Go Digital! *Use the online visual glossary*

(t to b, l to r) Catalin Petolea/Alamy; Losevsky Pavel/Alamy; FoodCollection/SuperStock; Huntstock/Getty Images; Comstock/Getty Images; Royalty-Free/Corbis; Dana Hoff/Photographer's Choice RF/Getty Images; Transtock/SuperStock

or, oar, ore

The letters or, oar, and ore can make the sounds you hear at the end of **for**, **roar**, and **more**.

oar	**born**	**tore**
shorter	**store**	**board**
roaring	**wore**	**form**
sports	**north**	**before**

Olga and Aleksey Ivanov

Read Together

Morty built a better board for the shore.

Are there some more at the sports store?

Your Turn

COLLABORATE

Look for these words with or, oar, and ore in "The Story of a Robot Inventor."

story **born** **sorts** **forms** **more**

short **for** **sports** **soar**

CCSS **Genre** Biography

Essential Question

What inventions do you know about?

Read about someone who invents robots.

Go Digital!

The Story of a Robot Inventor

Junko Kimura/Getty Images News/Getty Images

Big Ideas

Meet Tomotaka Takahashi. He invents **unusual** robots. How did he get started?

Mr. Takahashi was born in Japan in 1975. As a child, he played with blocks. He used his imagination to make all sorts of forms and shapes.

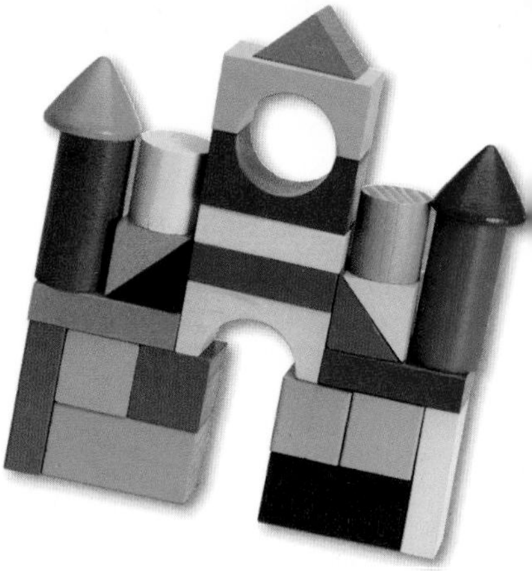

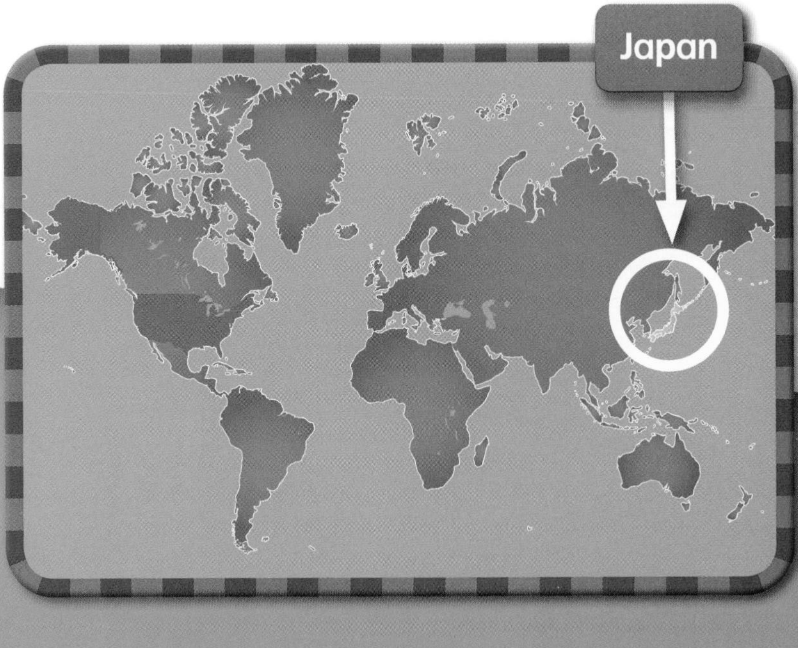

(t) Toru Yamanaka/AFP/Getty Images; (c) McGraw-Hill Companies/Ken Karp, photographer

Later, he read comic books about a robot named Astro Boy. The robot looked like a real child. Takahashi wanted to make robots just like it.

Photos 12/Alamy

Finding Out About Robots

In 1999, Takahashi **began** to study robots. He took classes to **learn** how they move. The robots bent their legs when they walked. It did not look **right** to Takahashi. People did not walk that way.

Then Takahashi had an **idea**. He made a **better** robot. It did not bend its legs when it walked. It moved more like a person.

Koichi Kamoshida/Getty Images News/Getty Images

Yoshikazu Tsuno/AFP/Getty Images

Making Better Robots

In 2003, Takahashi started his own company. He made many robots. A short robot climbed up a cliff with a rope. A bigger robot lifted a car with its arms. Another robot rode a bike for 24 hours.

Franck Robichon/EPA/Newscom

Takahashi began to put his robots in contests. He made three robots for a sports race in Hawaii in 2011. The first robot had to swim. The second robot had to ride a bike. The third robot had to run. The robots had to do these tasks for a week!

Toru Yamanaka/AFP/Getty Images

For the race, there were many problems to solve. Takahashi made the swimming robot waterproof. He gave it arms like fins to help it swim faster. Another robot was able to ride its bike for 100 miles without breaking. The third robot ran for 26 miles!

Toru Yamanaka/AFP/Getty Images

What will Takahashi invent next? Will his robots fly and soar like Astro Boy? Will they be his finest? We can only **guess**. We must wait and see.

Tomotaka Takahashi is **sure** of one thing. His robots will do more and more!

Make Connections

What kind of robot would you like to invent? **Essential Question**

Kyodo via AP Images

Problem and Solution

A **problem** is something that a person wants to do, change, or find out. The way the person solves the problem is the **solution**.

Find Text Evidence

Find one of the problems that Mr. Takahashi faced when building robots for the race.

page 167

Takahashi began to put his robots in contests. He made three robots for a sports race in Hawaii in 2011. The first robot had to swim. The second robot had to ride a bike. The third robot had to run. The robots had to do these tasks for a week!

Toru Yamanaka/AFP/Getty Images

Problem

Takahashi wanted to put a robot in a race where it had to swim.

Steps to Solution

He built a waterproof robot with arms like fins.

Solution

Takahashi built his robot in a way that it could swim.

COLLABORATE

Your Turn

Talk about the problems the inventor faced in "The Story of a Robot Inventor" and how he solved them.

Go Digital! *Use the interactive graphic organizer*

Readers to...

Word Choice Norm used time-order words to tell about a dance he invented.

Norm's Personal Narrative

I invented a new dance. First, I saw the greatest dancer on TV. Next, I practiced his steps. Then, I added new moves. I am a faster dancer than he is!

COLLABORATE

Your Turn

Tell what time-order words Norm used in his narrative. Which words will you use?

Read Together

Writers

Comparative Adjectives Add **-er** to most adjectives to compare two things. Add **-est** to compare more than two.

First, I saw the **greatest** dancer on TV. I am a **faster** dancer than he is!

Your Turn

- Tell what Norm is comparing in his narrative.
- Write new sentences. Use other adjectives that compare.

Olga and Aleksey Ivanov

Weekly Concept Sounds All Around

Essential Question

What sounds can you hear? How are they made?

Go Digital!

Listen Up!

Talk About It

How are these children making sounds?

CCSS Words to Know

color

This bird is a bright **color**.

early

Early morning can be very quiet.

instead

I try to whisper **instead** of shouting.

nothing

There is **nothing** in that can.

oh

Oh, our marching band has a great sound!

thought

He **thought** the jet was much too loud.

scrambled

Goats **scrambled** up the rocks.

suddenly

The sky **suddenly** lit up brightly!

Your Turn

Read the sentence for each word. Then make up another sentence.

Go Digital! *Use the online visual glossary*

(t to b, l to r) Tim Laman/National Geographic/Getty Images; Ingram Publishing/SuperStock; Nancy R. Cohen/Photodisc/Getty Images; Eco Images/Universal Images Group/Getty Images; Gary Conner/Photolibrary/Getty Images; Brand X Pictures/PunchStock; Bruce & Jan Lichtenberger/SuperStock; NOAA Photo Library, NOAA Central Library; OAR/ERL/National Severe Storms Laboratory (NSSL)

ou, ow

The letters ou and ow can make the sound you hear in the middle of **found** and **down**.

loud	**now**	**ground**
brown	**shouted**	**growling**
frowned	**cloud**	**pound**
mouse	**around**	**towel**

Pablo Bernasconi

Read Together

We found a brown puppy in town.

It does not growl or make loud sounds!

Your Turn

COLLABORATE

Look for these words with ou and ow in "Now, What's That Sound?"

now	sound	out	house
bouncing	shouted	wow	
crown	down	sounds	

CCSS **Genre** Realistic Fiction

Essential Question

What sounds can you hear? How are they made?

Read about two children who hunt for a sound.

Go Digital!

Pablo Bernasconi

Now, What's That Sound?

Tap-tap-tap. Rat-a-tat-tat.

"What's that sound?" asked Gilbert. "It started **early** this morning. I **thought** it might stop, but it hasn't!"

"Let's check out the garage," said Marta. "I think Dad is making the sound."

Pablo Bernasconi

Dad was in the garage cutting a board with his saw.

Zing, zing, zing.

"This is not the sound," said Gilbert. "This sound is smoother."

"Let's find Gramps," said Marta. "He might be making the sound."

They quickly ran to the back of the house to find Gramps.

Pablo Bernasconi

Gramps was sweeping the deck with a broom.

Swish, swish, swish.

“No, this is not the sound,” said Gilbert. “This sound is much softer.”

"Let's find Ana **instead**," said Marta. "Maybe she's making the sound."

They found Ana in the driveway. Ana was bouncing a ball.

Bam. . . bam . . . bam.

Pablo Bernasconi

"No, this is not the sound," said Gilbert. "This sound is slower."

"This is hopeless!" sighed Marta.

Tap-tap-tap. Rat-a-tat-tat.

"There it is again," said Gilbert. He looked up at the tallest tree. **Suddenly**, he shouted. "**Oh**, wow! It's a bird!"

"Look at the **color** on its head," cried Marta. "It's red, like a red crown."

The bird **scrambled** up and down the tree.

Tap-tap-tap. Rat-a-tat-tat.

Pablo Bernasconi

"It's a woodpecker pecking for bugs," said Gilbert.

"Yes," said Marta. "And **nothing** else sounds like it!"

Tap-tap-tap! Rat-a-tat-tat!

Make Connections

How are the sounds around you made? **Essential Question**

Problem and Solution

A **problem** is something characters want to do, change, or find out. The way the problem is solved is the **solution**.

Find Text Evidence

Find the problem that the story characters need to solve.

page 182

Tap-tap-tap. Rat-a-tat-tat.

"What's that sound?" asked Gilbert. "It started **early** this morning. I **thought** it might stop, but it hasn't!"

"Let's check out the garage," said Marta. "I think Dad is making the sound."

Pablo Bernasconi

Read Together

Problem

Gilbert and Marta hear a new sound.

Steps to Solution

Check if Dad is making the sound.

Check if Gramps is making the sound.

Check if Ana is making the sound.

Solution

Gilbert and Marta discover that the sound is a woodpecker tapping on a tree.

COLLABORATE

Your Turn

Talk about the problem and solution in "Now, What's That Sound?"

Go Digital! *Use the interactive graphic organizer*

Readers to...

Sentence Fluency Howard wrote complete sentences to express his opinion.

Howard's Review

This story is about a sound. That funny bird is very loud! The story has an ending that will surprise you. I liked it!

Your Turn

COLLABORATE

- Tell why the sentences in Howard's review are complete.
- What you will write an opinion about?

Read Together

Writers

Other Adjectives Use **a, an, this,** and **that** to tell which one. Use **a, this,** and **that** before nouns that start with a consonant. Use **an** before nouns that start with a vowel.

This story is
about a sound.

Your Turn

COLLABORATE

- Find **a, an,** and **that** in Howard's writing. Which word comes before a noun that starts with a vowel?
- Write a new sentence using one of the words.

Pablo Bernasconi

Weekly Concept Build It!

Essential Question

How do things get built?

Go Digital!

Huntstock/Getty Images

TIME FOR KIDS®

Up It Goes!

Talk About It

What is this carpenter building?

How is he doing it?

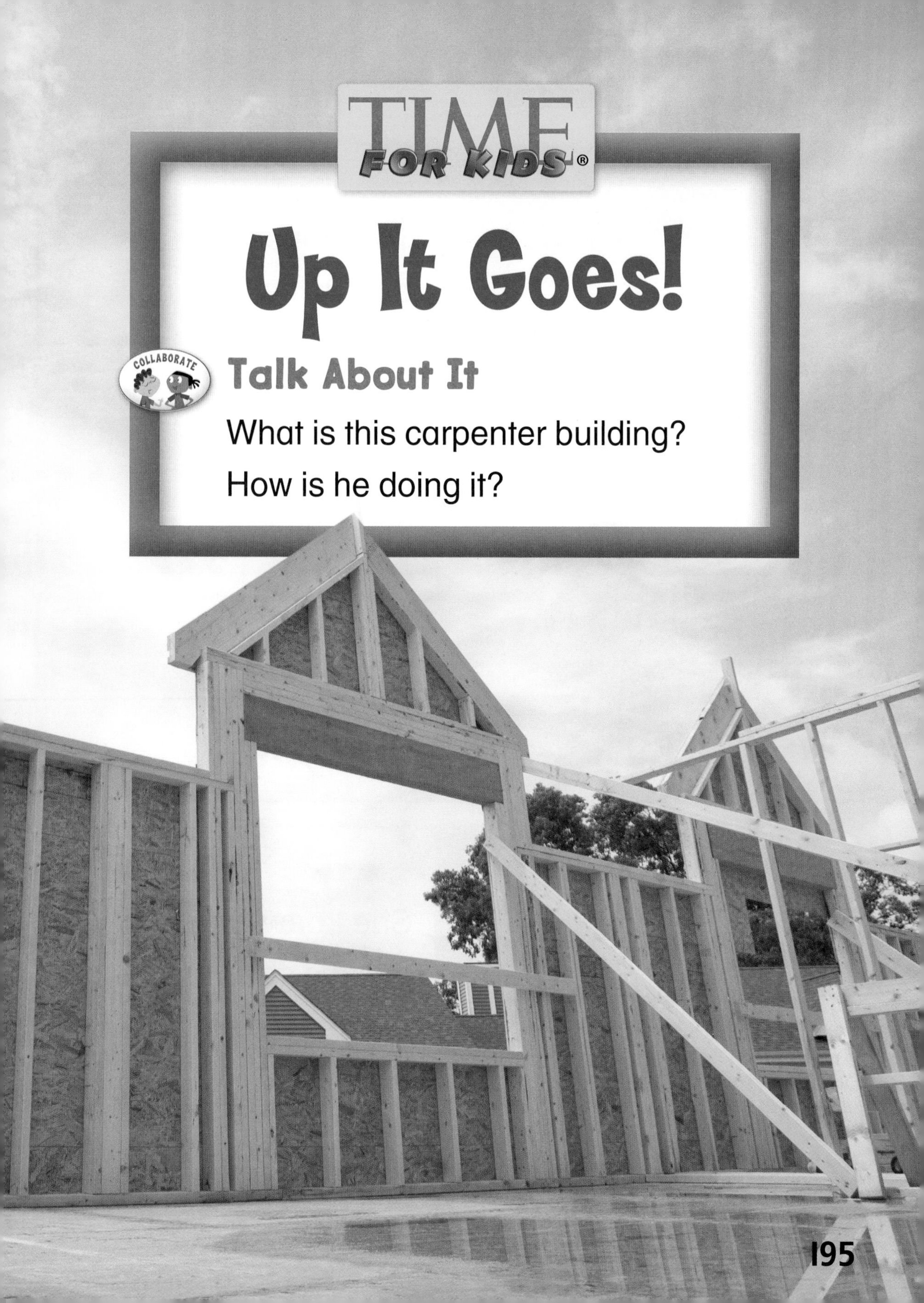

CCSS Words to Know

above

The cranes are **above** the building.

build

They will **build** some houses.

fall

It is strong and will not **fall**.

knew

She **knew** how to make a good model.

money

I put my **money** in a new bank.

toward

We walked **toward** the water.

balance

The worker can **balance** up high.

section

This **section** is not finished yet.

Your Turn

Read the sentence for each word. Then make up another sentence.

Go Digital! *Use the online visual glossary*

oy, oi

The letters oy and oi can make the sound you hear in the middle of **toys** and **point**.

oil	**joined**	**boiling**
boy	**hoist**	**enjoy**
moist	**employ**	**choice**
annoys	**noise**	**destroy**

Read Together

Let's avoid annoying this boy.

He does not enjoy the noise!

Your Turn

COLLABORATE

Look for these words with oy and oi in "The Joy of a Ship."

joy **employs** **hoist**

avoid **boils** **joins**

joints **point** **moist**

CCSS **Genre** Nonfiction

TIME FOR KIDS®

Essential Question

How do things get built?

Read about building a ship.

Go Digital!

Engel & Gielen/VISUM/The Image Works

The Joy of a Ship

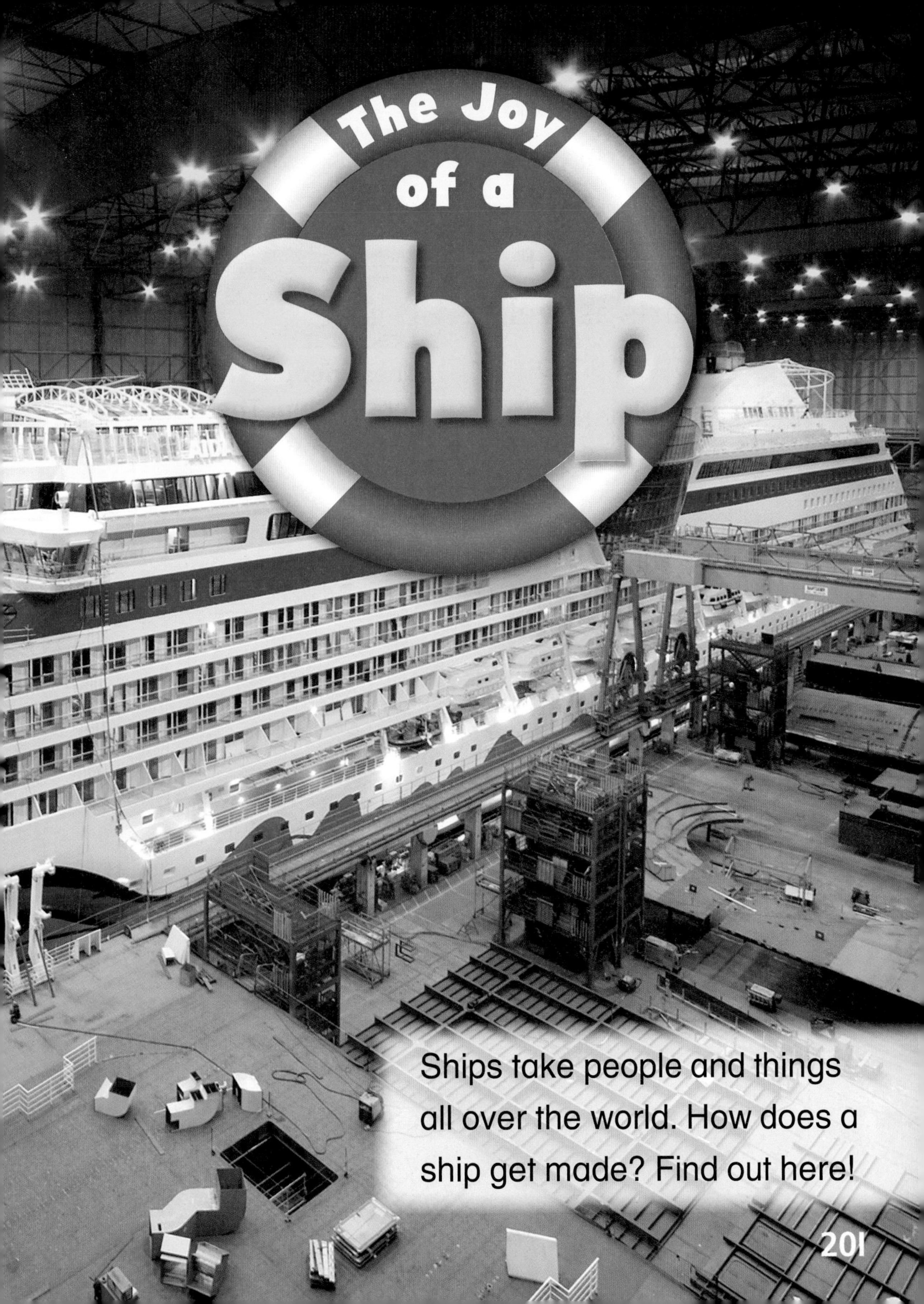

Ships take people and things all over the world. How does a ship get made? Find out here!

What is needed to **build** a ship? Making ships employs many workers. This task uses lots of tools and parts as well. Let's see how a ship is made, step by step.

These people study the plans for the ship. There are many things to do!

(t) Monty Rakusen/Cultura/Newscom; (b) Imaginechina/Corbis

Frame It!

First, workers build a frame. The ship frame can **balance** on blocks up **above** a dock. Huge cranes hoist the big parts in place so they do not **fall**. Workers must avoid being bumped by these big pieces of steel.

Some huge gantry cranes can lift 1,500 tons as high as 230 feet in the air.

Lo Mak/Redlink/Corbis

Sheets of Steel

First, two kinds of metal are melted into steel. It boils! Hot steel flows into flat metal sheets and molds. When steel gets cold, it gets hard. The steel sheets are then ready for making a ship.

Stand back! The steel is very hot!

Getty Images

A worker joins each steel **section** by heating the edges, called joints. Most workers put on gloves and a helmet to protect their hands and head.

Check It, Paint It

Workers check all the joints. Then they point out leaks and fix them. If a joint leaks, the inside of this ship will be moist with water. It might even sink!

Fritz Hoffmann/In Pictures/Corbis

Then, the ship is painted, and this job is done! It gleams in the sun. The workers **knew** it would look nice! People will pay a lot of **money** to ride on this ship.

Markus Hibbeler/AFP/Getty Images

Out to Sea!

The people on the dock point with joy as the new ship begins the first trip! Those on the ship wave as it glides **toward** the open sea.

Handout/Getty Images Entertainment/Getty Images

Did you know?

There are many kinds of ships on the sea.

Ice Breaker Ship ▼

Aircraft Carrier ▼

Cargo Ship ▼

Make Connections

What steps in ship building are risky? **Essential Question**

(bl) Purestock/SuperStock; (tr) USCG photo by Patrick Kelley; (br) BananaStock/Jupiterimages

Cause and Effect

A **cause** is how or why something happens. An **effect** is what happens.

Find Text Evidence

Find what causes hot steel to get hard.

page 204

First, two kinds of metal are melted into steel. It boils! Hot steel flows into flat metal sheets and molds. When steel gets cold, it gets hard. The steel sheets are then ready for making a ship.

Cause	Effect
Hot steel gets cold.	The steel gets hard.
A worker wears a helmet and gloves.	The worker's head and hands are safe.
A joint leaks on a ship.	The ship gets moist with water. It might sink.

COLLABORATE

Your Turn

Talk about what happens in "The Joy of a Ship" and how or why it happens.

Go Digital! *Use the interactive graphic organizer*

Readers to...

Organization Roy listed the steps in order in his writing.

Roy's How-to Article

First, make a flat spot in the snow. Next, make lots of big snowballs. Then, roll them toward the flat spot. Stack them. Now you have a snow fort!

Your Turn

COLLABORATE

What words did Roy use to tell the order of steps in his article?

Writers

Prepositions Words such as **toward, in, of, on, above, for, during,** and **beyond** link nouns to other words in a sentence.

Then, roll them **toward** the flat spot.

COLLABORATE

Your Turn

- Find more prepositions in Roy's writing.
- Write new sentences with prepositions. Circle the preposition in each sentence.

Unit 6

Together We Can!

LWA/Photographer's Choice/Getty Images

Together

Together is better,
Whatever we do,

You get so much more done,
When someone helps you.

If someone is lonely,
And not having fun,
Just ask them to play;

Two is better than one.

And books sound much better,
When shared with a friend,

Together is better,
Beginning to end.

—by Constance A. Kareme

The Big Idea

How does teamwork help us?

Weekly Concept Taking Action

Essential Question

How can we work together to make our lives better?

Go Digital!

Make It Happen!

COLLABORATE

Talk About It

What are these people working on together?

CCSS Words to Know

answer

I know the **answer** to that question!

brought

We all **brought** food for the picnic.

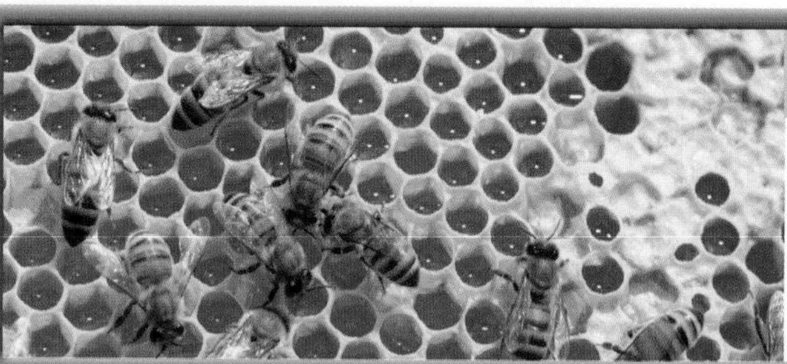

busy

The bees are **busy** making honey.

door

Grandpa met us at the **door**.

enough

Are there **enough** seats for all?

Read Together

eyes

Our **eyes** and ears help us learn.

demand

People can **demand** fair pay.

emergency

A fire is one kind of **emergency**.

Your Turn

COLLABORATE

Read the sentence for each word.
Then make up another sentence.

Go Digital! Use the online visual glossary

CCSS **Phonics/Fluency**

oo, u, u_e, ew, ue, ui, ou

The letters oo, u, u_e, ew, ue, ui, and ou can make the sound you hear in the middle of **cool**, **truth**, **flute**, **news**, **clues**, **suit**, and **soup**.

moon	**June**	**student**
flew	**true**	**fruit**
you	**room**	**July**
rude	**group**	**chewing**

Gynux

Read Together

Lucy and a group of friends sat by the pool.

Lucy, Sue, and Drew ate fruit.

Your Turn

Look for these words with oo, u, u_e, ew, ue, ui, and ou in "Super Tools."

super	**tools**	**few**	**new**
cool	**Lucy**	**used**	**useless**
rude	**soon**	**juice**	**drew**
blue	**you**	**room**	**useful**

Genre Fantasy

Essential Question

How can we work together to make our lives better?

Read about how a girl's forgotten writing tools work together to become useful again.

Go Digital!

Gynux

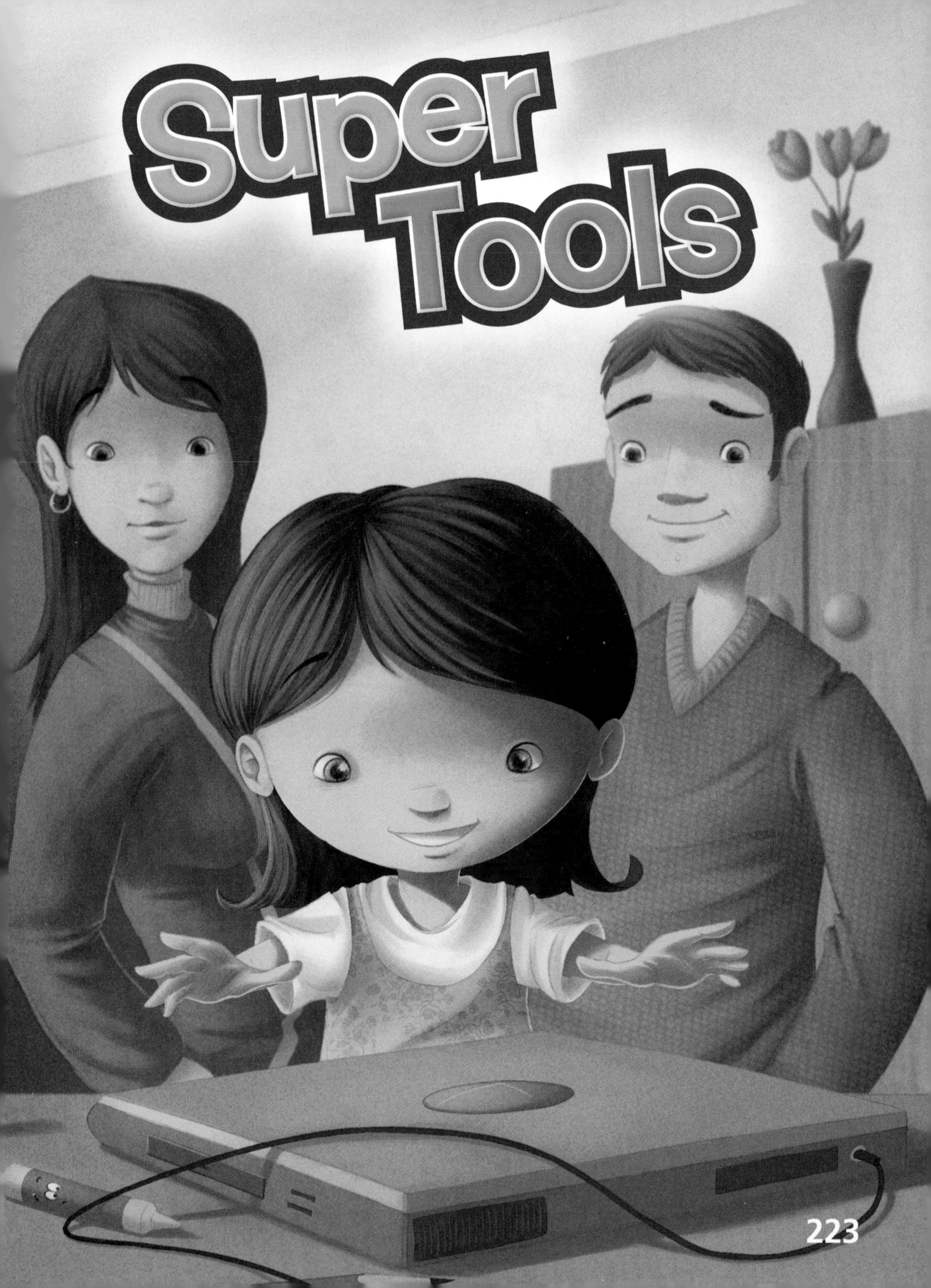
Super Tools

A few weeks ago, Lucy's mom and dad **brought** a new computer home. "This is so cool!" exclaimed Lucy. Lucy used the computer all the time.

But not everyone was happy about the new computer.

Lucy didn't know it, but her writing tools felt sad and useless. One day while she was at school, they had an **emergency** meeting.

"Lucy hasn't used us in weeks!" cried the markers. "Can we **demand** to be used?" asked the crayons. "No, that would be rude. But, we can remind her how great we are," said the pencils. "Yes!" they all agreed. "Let's remind her."

After school, as soon as Lucy came through the **door**, she grabbed a glass of juice and went right to her computer. She had to write a report about birds.

The writing tools watched and waited. When Lucy was done, she printed her report.

Gynux

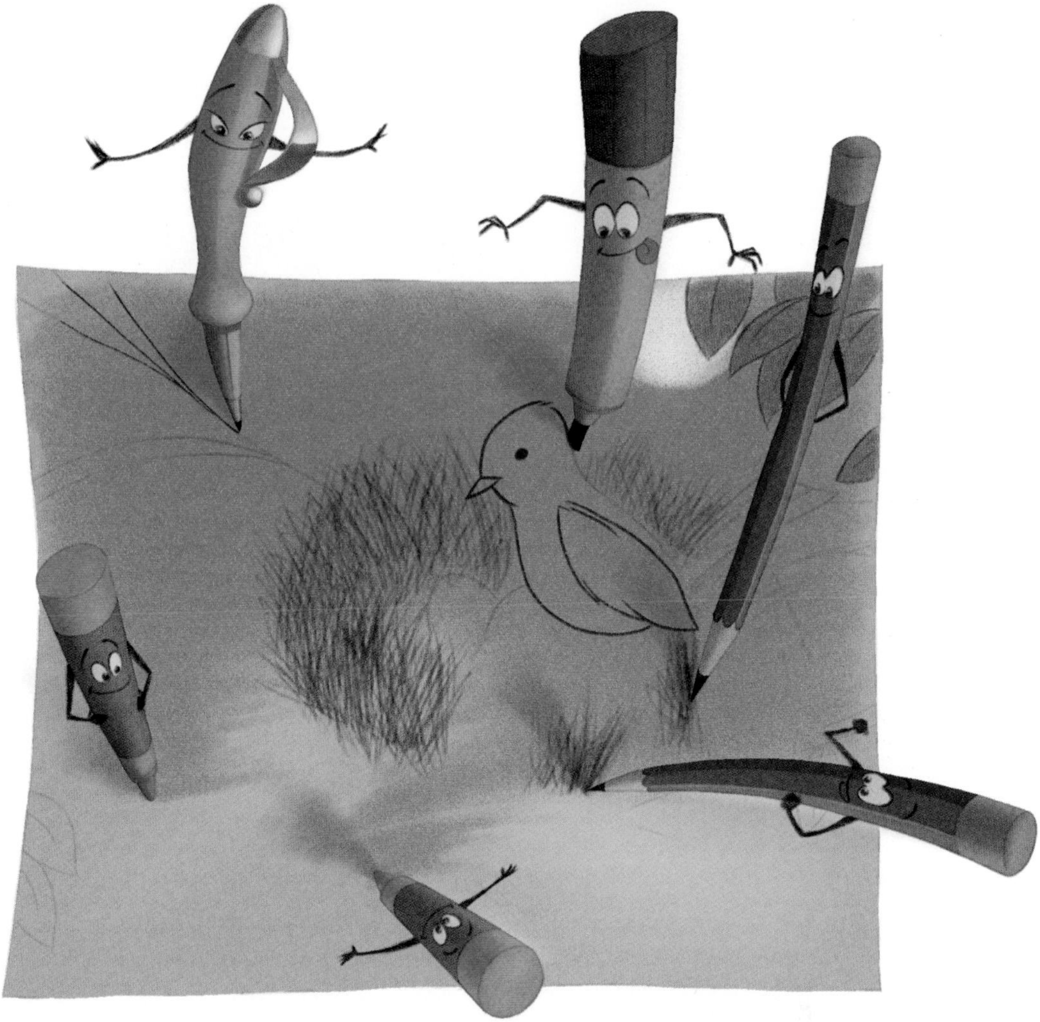

That night the writing tools got **busy**. They worked together to make a picture for Lucy.

The pencils made a sketch. The markers drew the birds in the tree. The crayons drew the sun in a blue sky. The picture was good **enough** to frame.

The next day was Saturday. Lucy woke up late. Then she went to get her report. Lucy gasped. She couldn't believe her **eyes**! "Who drew this great picture?" she asked.

Gynux

"Did you draw this?" Lucy asked Mom and Dad.
"You know the **answer** to that!" they laughed.
"Stop joking! YOU drew that great picture."

That made Lucy think she wished she had drawn it. "It is fun to draw," she said.

Lucy hung the picture in her room. Then she took out her pencils, crayons, and markers. "I'll draw my own picture for my report," she said.

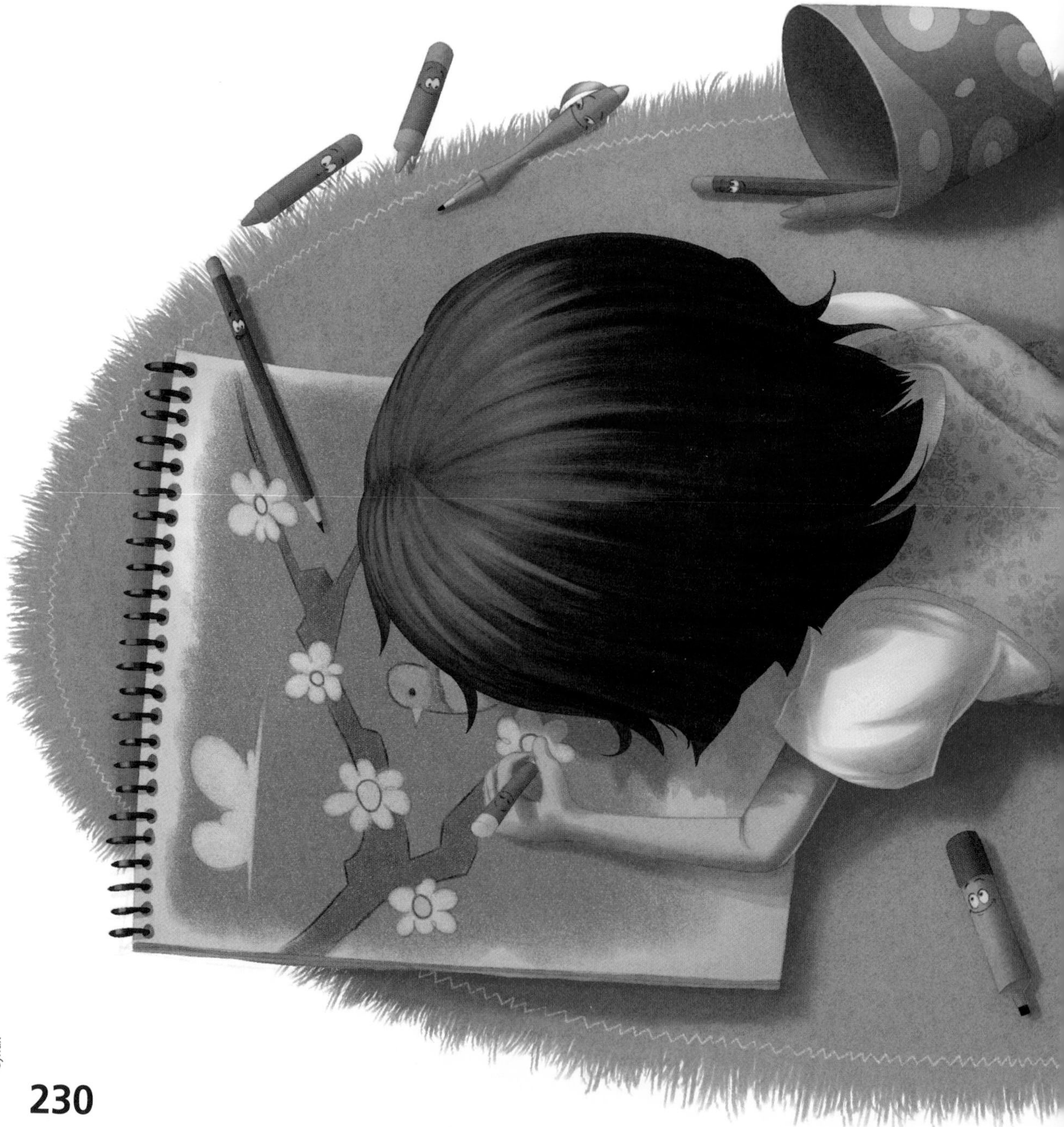

Gynux

Lucy and her pencils, crayons, and markers worked together. They drew a super picture.

From that day on, Lucy kept drawing. And the writing tools felt happy and useful!

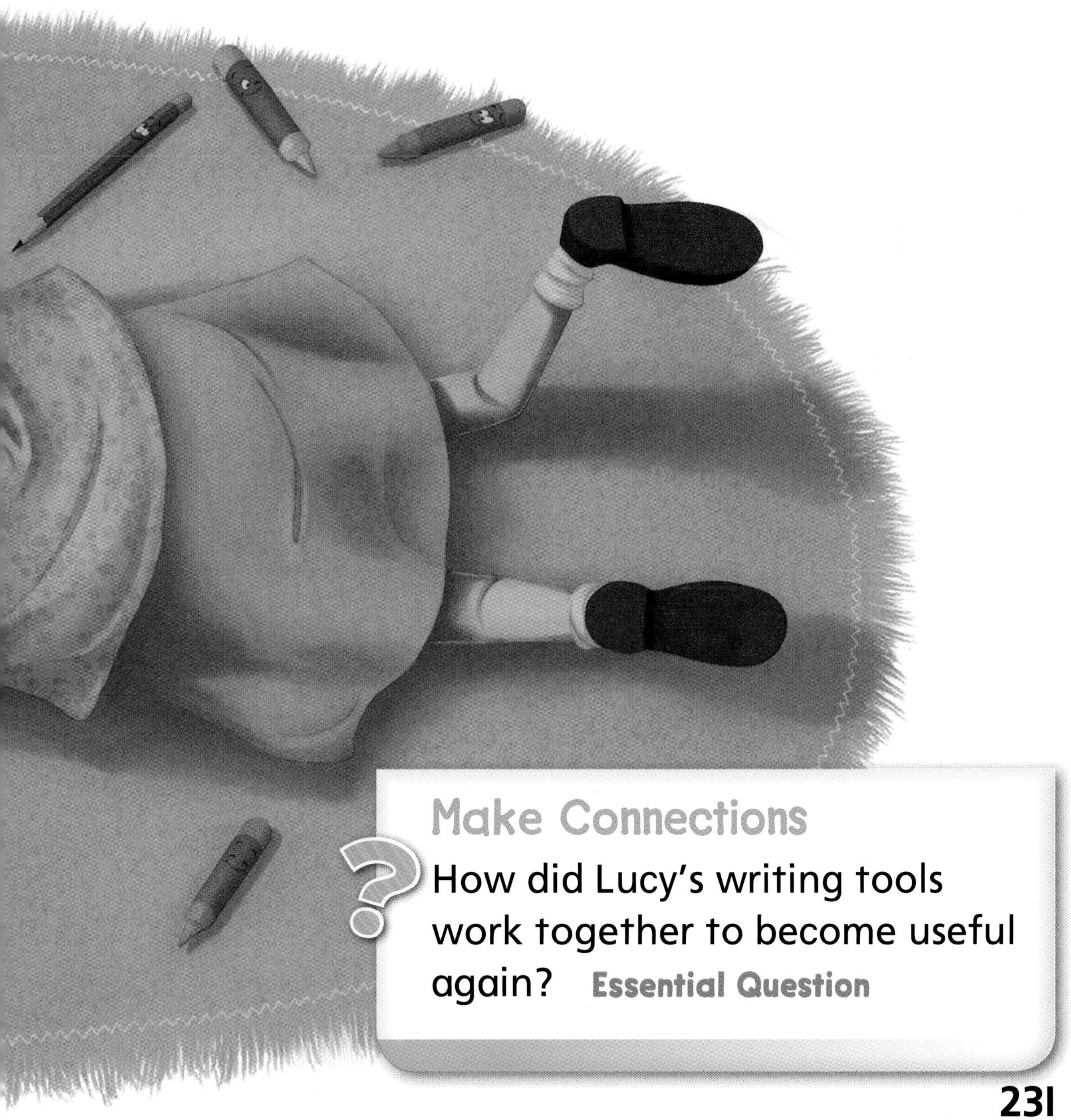

Make Connections

How did Lucy's writing tools work together to become useful again? **Essential Question**

Theme

The **theme** is the big idea or message of a story.

Find Text Evidence

Find clues that help you understand the theme.

page 227

That night the writing tools got **busy**. They worked together to make a picture for Lucy.

The pencils made a sketch. The markers drew the birds in the tree. The crayons drew the sun in a blue sky. The picture was good **enough** to frame.

Gynux

Read Together

Clue

The pencils made a sketch.

Clue

The markers drew the birds in the tree.

Clue

The crayons drew the sun in a blue sky.

Theme

The writing tools worked together to make their lives better.

COLLABORATE

Your Turn

Talk about the theme of "Super Tools."

Go Digital! *Use the interactive graphic organizer*

Readers to...

Sentence Fluency Sue used different kinds of sentences in her story.

Sue's Story

Ruby wanted to clean up the forest, so she called Rudy for help. "I will help you!" said Rudy. He got a big trash can and made a sign. It said, "Keep the forest clean!"

Your Turn

COLLABORATE

Tell how Sue varied the sentences in her story.

Read Together

Writers

Pronouns such as **I, you, he, she, it, we,** and **they** are words that take the place of nouns.

"**I** will help **you**!" said Rudy. **He** got a big trash can and made a sign.

COLLABORATE

Your Turn

- Find more pronouns in Sue's story.
- Write new sentences with pronouns. Circle the pronoun in each sentence.

Gynux

Weekly Concept My Team

Essential Question

Who helps you?

Go Digital!

LWA/The Image Bank/Getty Images

My Helpers

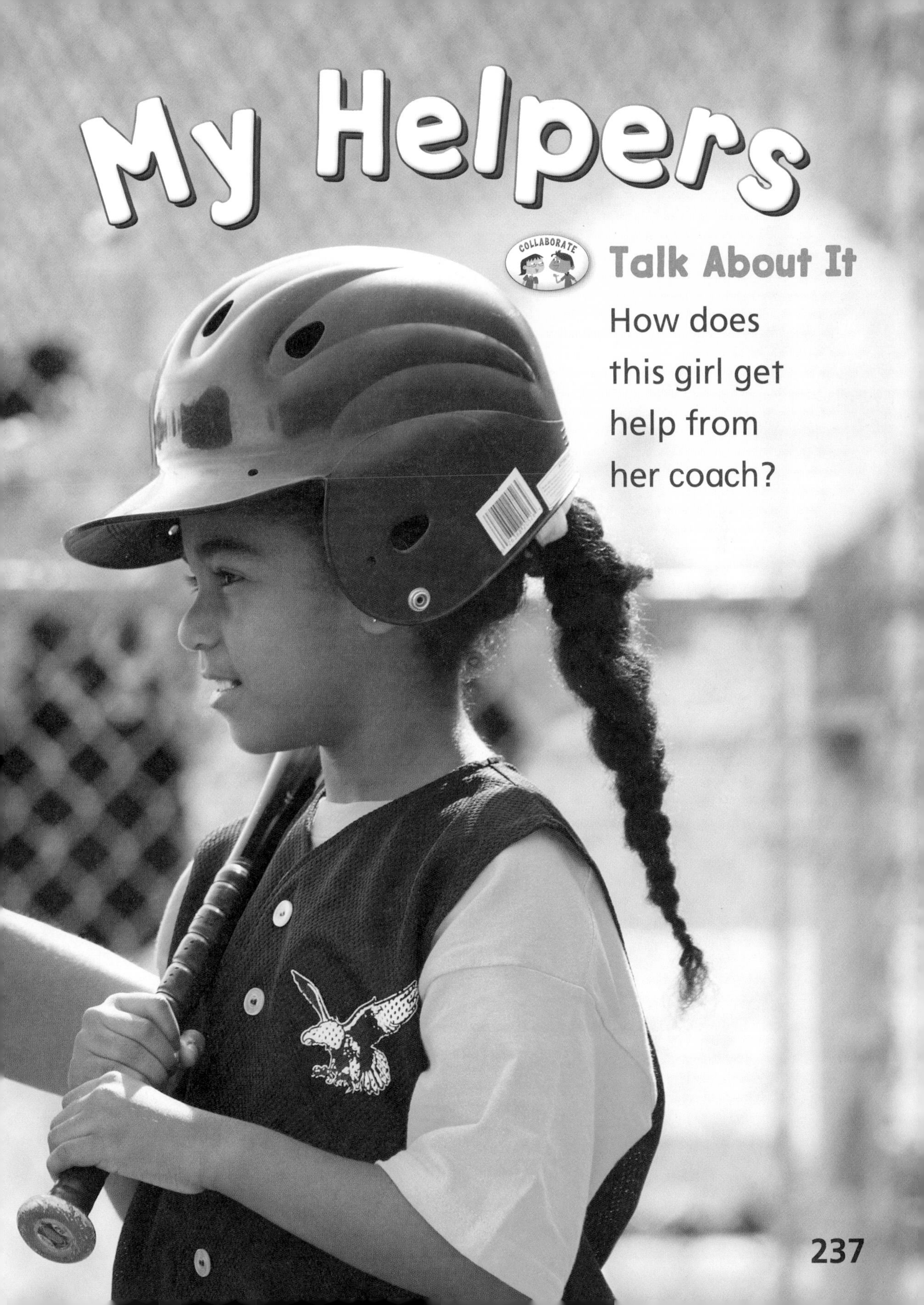

Talk About It

How does this girl get help from her coach?

Words to Know

brother

I like to read to my **brother**.

father

My **father** shows me how to swim.

friend

It's fun to have a good **friend**!

love

My family and I **love** each other.

mother

Pam's **mother** is our soccer coach.

picture

I drew a **picture** for my teacher.

accept

Will you **accept** this gift?

often

We **often** go to the library.

COLLABORATE

Your Turn

Read the sentence for each word.
Then make up another sentence.

Go Digital! *Use the online visual glossary*

(t to b, l to r) Reed Kraestner Photography; Comstock Images/Jupiter Images/Alamy; JGI/Jamie Gril/Blend Images/Getty Images; Tom Merton/OJO Images/Getty Images; UpperCut Images/SuperStock; Steven Puetzer/Digital Vision/Getty Images; fStop/SuperStock; Exactostock/SuperStock

a, aw, au, augh, al

The letters a, aw, au, augh, and al stand for the sound you hear in the middle of **calls**, **fawn**, **cause**, **caught**, and **walk**.

ball	**talking**	**haul**
saw	**salt**	**taught**
fault	**smallest**	**yawn**
also	**pause**	**daughter**

Read Together

Last fall, I taught Paul how to draw.

He drew a tall tree using chalk.

Your Turn

COLLABORATE

Look for these words with a, aw, au, augh, and al in "All Kinds of Helpers."

all	also	baseball	ball
talks	taught	awful	because
caught	walk	always	talk

CCSS **Genre** Nonfiction

Essential Question

Who helps you?

Read about the people in your community who help you and the different ways they help.

Go Digital!

All Kinds of Helpers

Every day, people help us in many ways. To help means to give what is needed and useful. It also means to make things better. So helpers are the people who give us what we need and who make our lives better.

Who are some of the people who help us?

Jupiterimages/Comstock Images/Getty Images

Families can be helpers. The people in a family **love** and **accept** us. They also help us in many ways.

A family can include a **mother** and a **father**. This boy also has a big **brother**. His brother **often** helps him with his homework. His mother and father help him learn about the world.

Corbis/age fotostock

Teachers help you in many ways. In school, a teacher helps you learn how to read and write. A teacher teaches you such subjects as math and social studies. A teacher helps you understand new ideas.

Big Cheese Photo/Alamy

Sports coaches are helpers, too. The baseball coach in this **picture** is teaching his team how to hold the ball. He talks to them and shows them what to do. Who taught you how to play a sport?

LWA/The Image Bank/Getty Images

Doctors and nurses help keep you healthy. You visit the doctor for a checkup or when you feel sick.

The girl in this picture feels awful because she caught a bad cold! But the doctor will help her get better.

Image Source/Getty Images

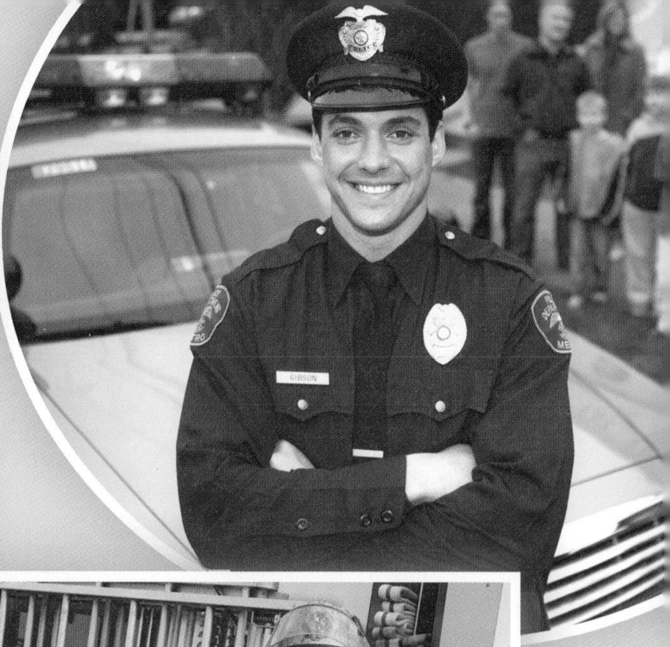

Do you walk or take a bus to school? Either way, people help you get back and forth safely.

Other helpers keep you safe, too. Police officers and firefighters are always protecting you.

(l) moodboard/Alamy; (tr) Masterfile; (br) Skip Nall/Corbis

Some boys and girls need a grownup to talk to. Some groups match boys and girls with a grownup who will be their **friend**. What a good idea!

A special group called **Big Brothers Big Sisters** helps some children out.

Alistair Berg/Digital Vision/Getty Images

There are many helpers around you. Families love you, and teachers help you learn. Doctors, nurses, and safety helpers keep you healthy and safe. Special groups help you in special ways. All of them give what is needed and useful.

Comstock/PunchStock

Make Connections

Who are the people in your community that help you? How do they help? **Essential Question**

Author's Purpose

The **author's purpose** is the reason why an author writes a selection.

Find Text Evidence

Find a clue to help you understand the author's purpose.

page 251

There are many helpers around you. Families love you, and teachers help you learn. Doctors, nurses, and safety helpers keep you healthy and safe. Special groups help you in special ways. All of them give what is needed and useful.

Read Together

Clue	Clue
Families love you, and teachers help you learn.	Doctors, nurses, and safety helpers keep you healthy and safe.

Author's Purpose

To let you know that there are many people helping you in many ways.

COLLABORATE

Your Turn

Talk about the author's purpose for writing "All Kinds of Helpers."

Go Digital! *Use the interactive graphic organizer*

CCSS **Writing and Grammar**

Readers to...

Voice Paul chose words that make his thank-you note sound friendly.

Paul's Thank-You Note

Dear Gram,

Thank you for my new puppy. His name is Buddy. I hope Buddy is as smart as your dog!

Love, Paul

COLLABORATE

Your Turn

What possessive pronouns did Paul use in his thank-you note?

Read Together

Writers

Possessive pronouns such as **my, your, his, her, its, our,** and **their** can take the place of possessive nouns.

Thank you for **my** new puppy. **His** name is Buddy.

COLLABORATE

Your Turn

- Find another possessive pronoun in Paul's thank-you note.
- Write new sentences with possessive pronouns. Circle the possessive pronoun in each sentence.

Robin Boyer

Weekly Concept Weather Together

Essential Question

How can weather affect us?

Go Digital!

Derek Croucher/Alamy

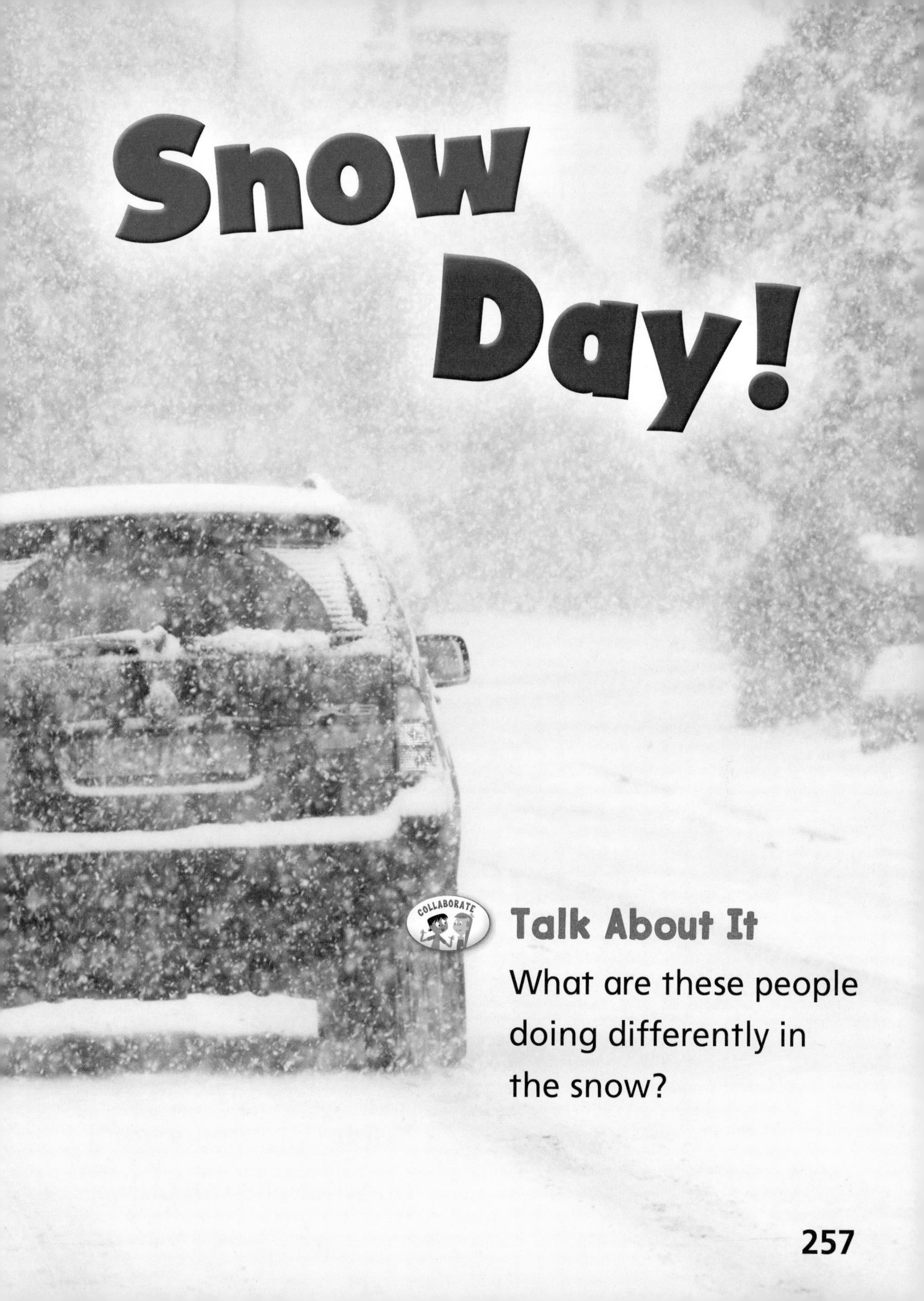

Snow Day!

Talk About It

What are these people doing differently in the snow?

Words to Know

been

They have **been** busy raking.

children

The **children** won their last game of the year.

month

July can be a very hot **month**.

question

Who will answer the **question**?

their

Their dog likes to cool off when it's hot out!

Read Together

year

It snowed a lot here this **year**.

country

This is a map of our **country**.

gathers

She **gathers** some spring flowers.

COLLABORATE

Your Turn

Read the sentence for each word. Then make up another sentence.

***Go Digital!** Use the online visual glossary*

Silent Letters wr, kn, gn

Sometimes a letter is silent. The letters wr, kn, and gn make the sound you hear at the beginning of **wrap**, **know**, and **gnat**.

write	**sign**	**knot**
knee	**gnawed**	**wreck**
gnat	**knocking**	**wrist**
knife	**wreath**	**design**

Peter Francis

I knocked a gnat off my wrist.

Another bug gnawed on my knee!

Your Turn

COLLABORATE

Look for these words with wr, kn, and gn in "Wrapped in Ice."

wrapped	**design**	**know**	**signs**
knocked	**Knox**	**Wright**	**knock**

CCSS **Genre** Realistic Fiction

Essential Question

How can weather affect us?

Read how icy weather affects a neighborhood.

Go Digital!

Peter Francis

Wrapped in Ice

The sound of something hitting the window woke Kim up. *Ping! Ping, ping!* "What's that?" Kim asked herself.

Kim peeked outside. The trees were coated with ice. The yard sparkled. The driveway was like a skating rink. Even the car was wrapped in an icy design.

Peter Francis

"Mom, why is everything covered in ice?" Kim wanted to know.

"That's a good **question**," said Mom. "Good thing I'm a science teacher! It's raining. But the air is very cold. So the raindrops freeze when they land on cold surfaces like signs, trees, and roads."

Mom turned on the TV weather. A reporter said, "A winter storm has hit this part of the **country**. Freezing rain is making streets and roads icy. We advise you to stay inside! **Children** can stay home. Schools will be closed."

"We have a snow day!" cried Kim.
"You mean an ice day!" laughed Mom.

Peter Francis

Suddenly, all the lights went out!

"I guess some icy tree branches broke," said Mom. "They must have knocked down power lines. We won't have any power until the lines are fixed."

Kim looked worried. But Mom said, "Let's just pretend we are camping!"

Mom lit the logs in the fireplace. Kim got flashlights. They played lots of games. It was fun to eat **their** lunch by the fire.

Then Mom said, "Listen!" The *ping, ping, ping* had stopped!

"The storm must be over!" cried Kim.

Peter Francis

Up and down the street, people came outside. There was so much to do. Everyone worked together. They put sand on the walks. They broke up the ice. Noses got red. Br-r-r-r! The air was very cold.

"I made a fire in the fireplace," Mom called out. "Come in and warm up!"

Neighbors came with flashlights and snacks. Ms. Knox brought cider. Mr. Wright told about the **year** it snowed in the **month** of May. Kim told knock-knock jokes.

"It's nice when everyone **gathers** together," said Mom.

Peter Francis

Just then, the lights came on. Everyone cheered.

"It's **been** a big day!" smiled Mom. "We were lucky to be cozy and safe."

"We are lucky to have such nice neighbors, too," said Kim. "We turned an ice day into an ice party!"

Make Connections

How does icy weather change Kim and her neighborhood?

Essential Question

Cause and Effect

A **cause** is the reason why something happens. An **effect** is what happens.

Find Text Evidence

Find what caused the raindrops to freeze.

page 265

"Mom, why is everything covered in ice?" Kim wanted to know.

"That's a good **question**," said Mom. "Good thing I'm a science teacher! It's raining. But the air is very cold. So the raindrops freeze when they land on cold surfaces like signs, trees, and roads."

Peter Francis

Read Together

Cause	Effect
The air was very cold.	Raindrops froze on cold surfaces.
Branches broke. Power lines fell.	There was no electricity.
The air was very cold.	Noses got red.

COLLABORATE

Your Turn

Talk about what happened in "Wrapped in Ice" and what caused it to happen.

Go Digital! *Use the interactive graphic organizer*

Readers to...

Voice Judy chose words to make her letter sound friendly.

Judy's Letter

Dear Mark,

Everyone thinks snow is fun. Not me! Our van got stuck last night. Nobody came by. Then a tow truck stopped. Hooray!

Your pal, Judy

Your Turn

Tell what words gave Judy's letter a friendly voice.

Read Together

Writers

Indefinite Pronouns Pronouns such as **everyone, nobody, everything**, and **nothing** do not name one special thing.

Everyone thinks snow is fun.

Your Turn

- Find a pronoun in Judy's letter that stands for "no person."
- Write new sentences with **everyone, nobody, everything**, or **nothing.**

Peter Francis

Weekly Concept Sharing Traditions

Essential Question

What traditions do you know about?

Go Digital!

Talk About It

What is this boy learning from his grandmother?

(bkgd) Monalyn Gracia/Corbis; (inset) The McGraw-Hill Companies, Inc./Jacques Cornell photographer

Pass It On!

CCSS Words to Know

before

They read **before** going to bed.

front

The dog walks in **front** of the girl.

heard

Have you **heard** Dad play?

push

Mom will **push** the sled.

tomorrow

I hope it will be sunny **tomorrow**.

your

I'm glad to meet **your** mom!

difficult

This puzzle is **difficult** to do.

nobody

Nobody is on the porch.

COLLABORATE

Your Turn

Read the sentence for each word. Then make up another sentence.

Go Digital! Use the online visual glossary

(t to b, l to r) Yellow Dog Productions/Getty Images; Profimedia International s.r.o./Alamy; Somos Images/Corbis; ableimages/SuperStock; Purestock/Getty Images; SW Productions/Brand X/Corbis; Jose Luis Pelaez/Iconica/Getty Images; VisionsofAmerica.com/Joe Sohm/Getty Images

Three-Letter Blends

The letters scr, spl, spr, str, thr, and shr make the beginning sounds in **scramble**, **split**, **spring**, **stripes**, **three**, and **shrink**.

scrub	**sprayed**	**street**
splash	**shrink**	**thrilling**
spread	**scream**	**thread**
shriek	**splinters**	**strike**

Hector Borlasca

Read Together

A stream of water sprayed and splashed us.

The thrill made us shriek and scream.

Your Turn

COLLABORATE

Look for these words with scr, spl, spr, str, thr, and shr in "A Spring Birthday."

spring	street	sprang
spread	striking	three
split	shrieked	scrambled

CCSS **Genre** Realistic Fiction

Essential Question

What traditions do you know about?

Read about how a family starts a new tradition.

Go Digital!

Hector Borlasca

A Spring Birthday

May was a happy time for Marco. It was his birthday month.

"Can I have a party this year?" he asked. "Then my friends can celebrate with me."

Hector Borlasca

"It's our family tradition to have a birthday dinner," said Gram. "**Your** friends can join us. I will make *empanadas* for everyone."

"**Nobody** makes better *empanadas*, Gram!" Marco said. "But it would be fun to do something new this year."

"How about a picnic?" Dad asked. "I **heard** about a nice spot in the park on Elm Street. It's in **front** of the ball field. We can **push** the tables together."

"That sounds like fun," said Marco. "We can have hotdogs, burgers, and Gram's *empanadas*!"

Hector Borlasca

At last, it was the morning of Marco's birthday. He opened his eyes. He saw Mom and Dad and Gram. They were singing the Mexican birthday song, "*Las mañanitas.*" Marco sprang out of bed. He could not wait for his party.

Mom and Dad went shopping **before** the party. First, they got a baseball mitt for Marco. Then they bought a birthday cake and a *piñata*.

Everyone met at the picnic spot. "Happy birthday! *Feliz cumpleaños*, Marco!" they shouted.

Hector Borlasca

Mom hung the *piñata*. Dad spread out the food. There were hotdogs, burgers, and yummy *empanadas*!

After lunch, the children took turns striking the *piñata*. Each one swung three times. The *piñata* was **difficult** to hit! At last it split open. The kids shrieked and scrambled for the treats.

Hector Borlasca

Next Marco opened his gifts. When he saw the baseball mitt, he cried, "Thank you! This is just what I wanted! I can use it in the game **tomorrow**."

When it was time for cake, Marco's family sang the Mexican birthday song again. Marco's friends hummed along. Then Mom taught them the words so they could sing it, too!

"This is the best birthday party I've ever had!" Marco said. "Can we do this again next year?"

"Sure," said Gram. "It's fun to mix the old with the new. A spring picnic can be your birthday tradition."

Make Connections

What traditions do you know about from other places in the world? **Essential Question**

Theme

The **theme** of a story is the message that the author wants to tell readers.

Find Text Evidence

Find clues that can help you figure out the theme of "A Spring Birthday."

page 285

"It's our family tradition to have a birthday dinner," said Gram. "**Your** friends can join us. I will make *empanadas* for everyone."

"**Nobody** makes better *empanadas*, Gram!" Marco said. "But it would be fun to do something new this year."

Hector Borlasca

Read Together

Clue

A birthday dinner is the family's tradition.

Clue

Marco's family has a picnic with a *piñata*, *empanadas*, and other kinds of food.

Clue

Marco wants a birthday picnic next year.

Theme

Blend old and new to make a new tradition.

COLLABORATE

Your Turn

Talk about the theme of "A Spring Birthday."

Go Digital! *Use the interactive graphic organizer*

CCSS **Writing and Grammar**

Readers to...

Sentence Fluency Andy used different kinds of sentences to make his writing interesting.

Andy's Letter

Dear Trish,

Have you been to the zoo? I go each spring with Gramps. This year he bought me a toy seal! I had lots of fun.

Your friend, Andy

COLLABORATE

Your Turn

Tell what kinds of sentences Andy used in his letter.

Read Together

Writers

Using I and me Use **I** as the subject of a sentence. Use **me** after a verb or after a word such as **for, at, of, with, to,** or **between**.

I go each spring with Gramps.
This year he bought
me a toy seal!

COLLABORATE

Your Turn

- Find another place where Andy uses **I** or **me** in his writing. Tell why Andy used that word.
- Write new sentences. Use **I** and **me** in your sentences.

Hector Borlasca

Weekly Concept Celebrate America!

Essential Question

Why do we celebrate holidays?

Go Digital!

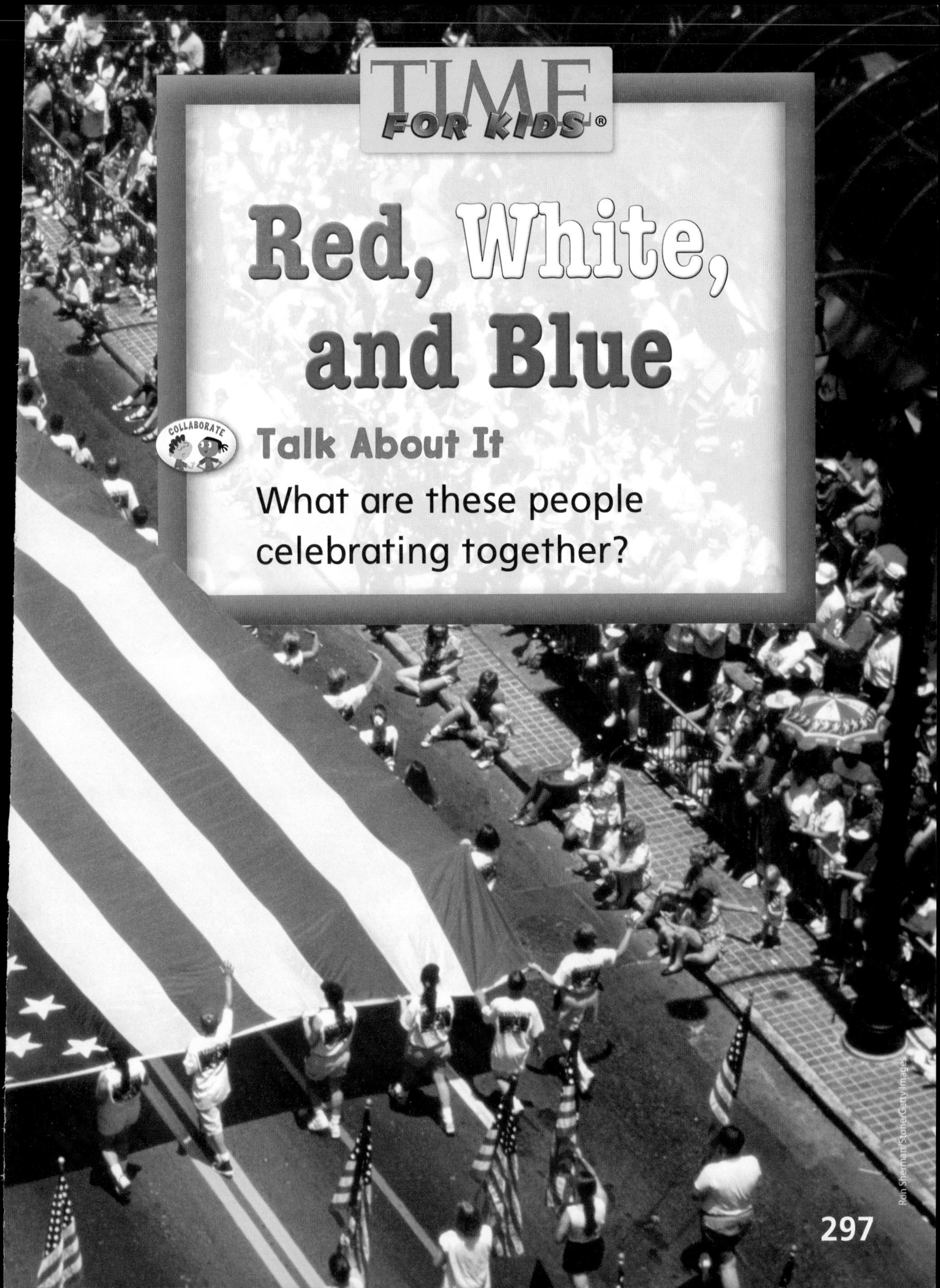

TIME FOR KIDS®

Red, White, and Blue

COLLABORATE

Talk About It

What are these people celebrating together?

Ron Sherman/Stone/Getty Images

Words to Know

favorite

It's my **favorite** day of the year!

few

A **few** of the apples are green.

gone

All the leaves are **gone**.

surprise

He has a **surprise** for his sister!

wonder

I **wonder** what is up in the tree.

young

The **young** child fell fast asleep.

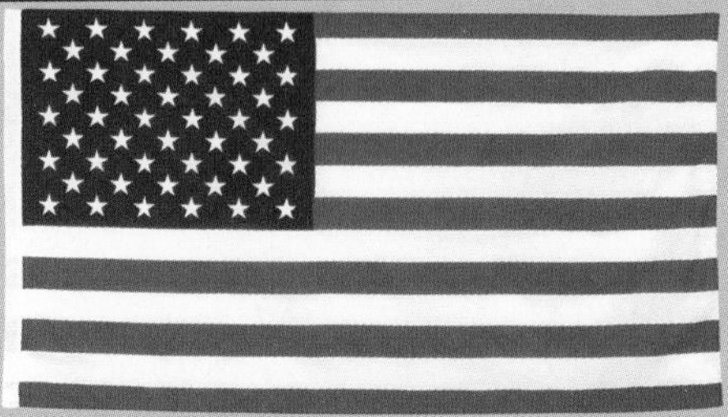

nation

Our **nation** has 50 states.

unite

We all **unite** to help the earth.

Your Turn

Read the sentence for each word. Then make up another sentence.

Go Digital! ***Use the online visual glossary***

air, are, ear

The letters air, are, and ear can make the sounds at the end of **fair**, **share**, and **pear**.

air	**care**	**hair**
bear	**pair**	**glare**
wear	**scare**	**chair**
stair	**square**	**aware**

Tim Beaumont

Read Together

A pair of chairs were at the square table.

She likes to wear a bow in her hair.

Your Turn

COLLABORATE

Look for these words with air, are, and ear in "Share the Harvest and Give Thanks."

share **fair** **aware** **compare**

affair **wear** **pears**

CCSS **Genre** Nonfiction

TIME FOR KIDS®

Essential Question

Why do we celebrate holidays?

Read about how people celebrate the harvest.

Go Digital!

Pierre Desrosiers/Photographer's Choice RF/Getty Images

Share the Harvest and Give Thanks

Each year, farmers pick crops from their fields. This is called the harvest. It marks the end of the growing season—a fun time of the year.

Say Thanks

In our **nation**, families celebrate the harvest in a number of ways. You can eat a harvest dinner at home, or you can go to a fair or festival. Harvest is a time to **unite** with friends and family. It is also a time when people share harvest foods.

Farm stands have harvest fruits and vegetables. These may include pumpkins and apples in the fall and berries and tomatoes in the spring.

(t) Karin Dreyer/Blend Images/Getty Images; (b) C Squared Studios/Photodisc/Getty Images

All across the United States, people give thanks for the fall harvest. This day is called Thanksgiving. It is on the fourth Thursday in November. Families eat together and show that they are thankful. But are you aware of the very first Thanksgiving?

Image Source/Getty Images

In 1620, the people we call Pilgrims sailed from England and landed in Plymouth, Massachusetts. The Native Americans there taught the Pilgrims which crops to plant.

The first Thanksgiving in our nation was in 1621. The Pilgrims who had come to America had a feast to show thanks for the harvest. They ate duck, deer, corn, and squash. Can you compare that to a meal today?

Bettmann/Corbis

Today, families still give thanks with a feast. But they may eat such **favorite** foods as turkey, corn, and green beans. People like to enjoy the harvest foods before they are **gone**.

Many families eat a special meal on Thanksgiving. Foods that are harvested in the fall may be part of the celebration.

Festivals and Fairs

In many states, Thanksgiving is a fun affair! Some places hold big parades where people march, sing, and dance. At one parade, **young** actors wear costumes. They act out the first Thanksgiving. That is so you can see what harvest was like so many years ago.

In Plymouth, the city of the first Thanksgiving, some people dress up like Pilgrims and Native Americans.

Michael Springer/Getty Images News/Getty Images

At the Kentucky Harvest Festival, the corn crop is the star. Kids have a contest to peel the most ears of corn. Families join teams to play a Cornhole Toss game. The teams toss a **few** bags filled with corn kernels. They follow rules to score. The winning team gets a **surprise**!

A bean-bag toss game is popular at Kentucky and Ohio harvest festivals. Players pitch their corn bags and try to get them into a hole.

Stan Rohrer/Alamy

Kwanzaa is also a harvest celebration. Kwanzaa means "first fruits." At this time, people give thanks for crops such as corn, apples, and pears.

In some places, pumpkins are a BIG deal! Large pumpkins are dug out and used as boats. After the race the pumpkins are used for compost, or to make new dirt.

Kwanzaa begins on December 26. It celebrates the harvest of Africa. Many people in the United States celebrate Kwanzaa traditions.

Row, row, row your pumpkin! These giant pumpkins make a splash at Oregon's Giant Pumpkin Race.

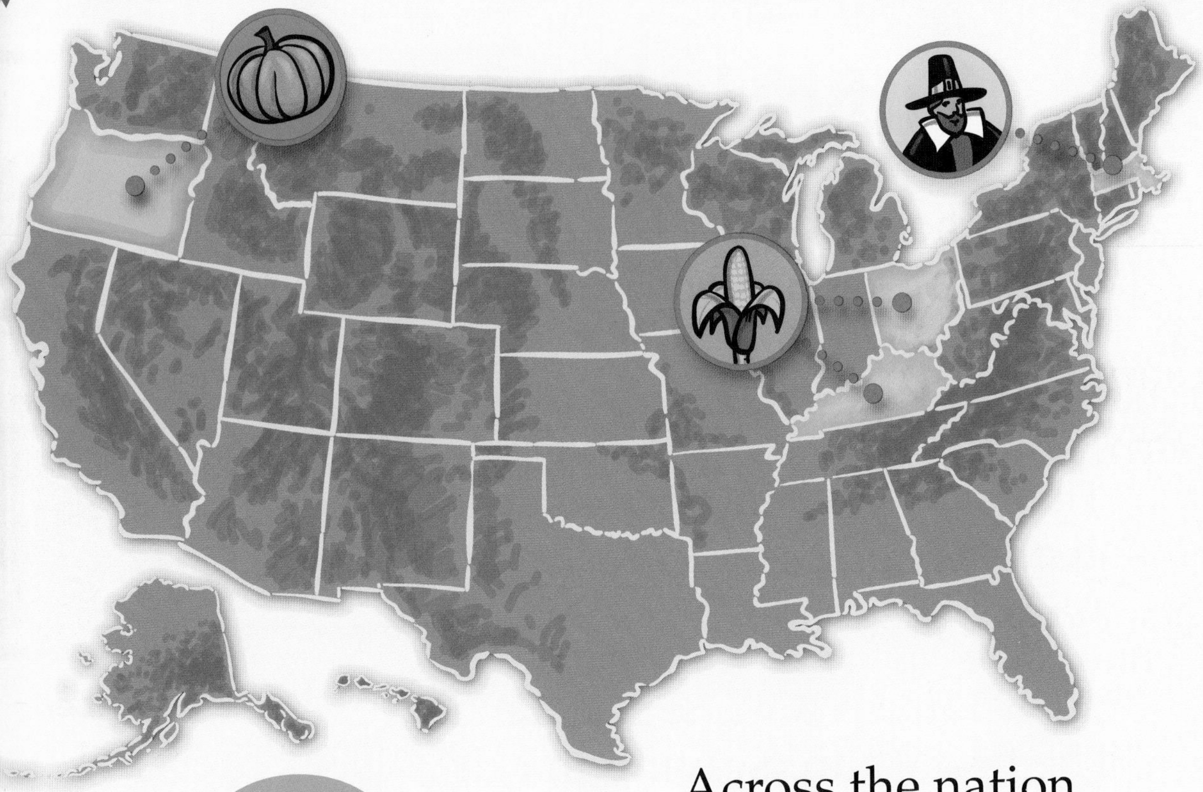

Across the nation, people celebrate the harvest. At home or with others, it is no **wonder** that harvest is a fun time for all!

Key

- Pumpkin Race in Oregon
- Corn Festivals in Kentucky and Ohio
- Pilgrims at the First Thanksgiving in Massachusetts

Make Connections

How do you celebrate the harvest? **Essential Question**

George Hamblin

Author's Purpose

An **author's purpose** is the reason why an author writes a selection.

Find Text Evidence

Find a clue to help you understand the author's purpose.

page 306

The first Thanksgiving in our nation was in 1621. The Pilgrims who had come to America had a feast to show thanks for the harvest. They ate duck, deer, corn, and squash. Can you compare that to a meal today?

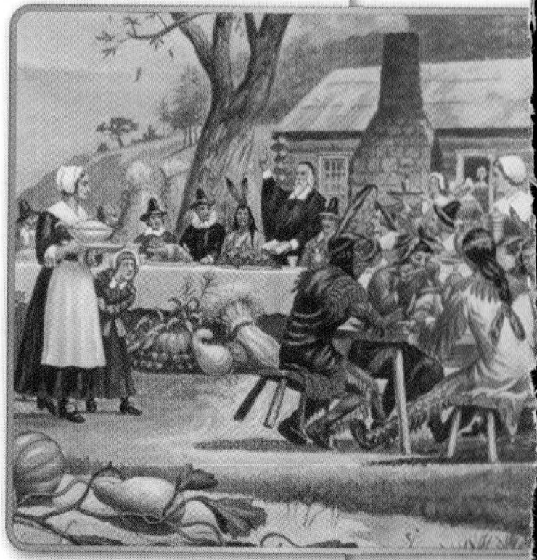

Bettmann/Corbis

Clue

The first Thanksgiving feast was in 1621 to show thanks for the harvest.

Clue

Today people still have feasts on Thanksgiving. There are also parades, fairs, and festivals.

Author's Purpose

To give information about the first Thanksgiving and how it is celebrated today.

Your Turn

Talk about the author's purpose for writing "Share the Harvest and Give Thanks."

Go Digital! ***Use the interactive graphic organizer***

Davies and Starr/Photodisc/Getty Images

Readers to...

Ideas Blair had an idea for a report. She used details to tell about her topic.

Blair's Report

Our nation's birthday is July 4. We celebrate with fireworks. The fireworks burst loudly. Big kids like them a lot. Little kids quickly cover their ears!

Your Turn

What details did Blair use in her report?

Read Together

Writers

Adverbs That Tell How Some adverbs tell how an action is done. Adverbs that tell how often end in **-ly**, such as **slowly**, **quickly**, **loudly**, **softly**, **neatly**, and **gladly**.

The fireworks burst **loudly**.

Your Turn

- Find another word in Blair's report that tells how an action is done.
- Write new sentences using words that tell how.

Tim Beaumont